GRASS ROOTS

BY STAN LYNDE

COTTONWOOD GRAPHICS, INC.

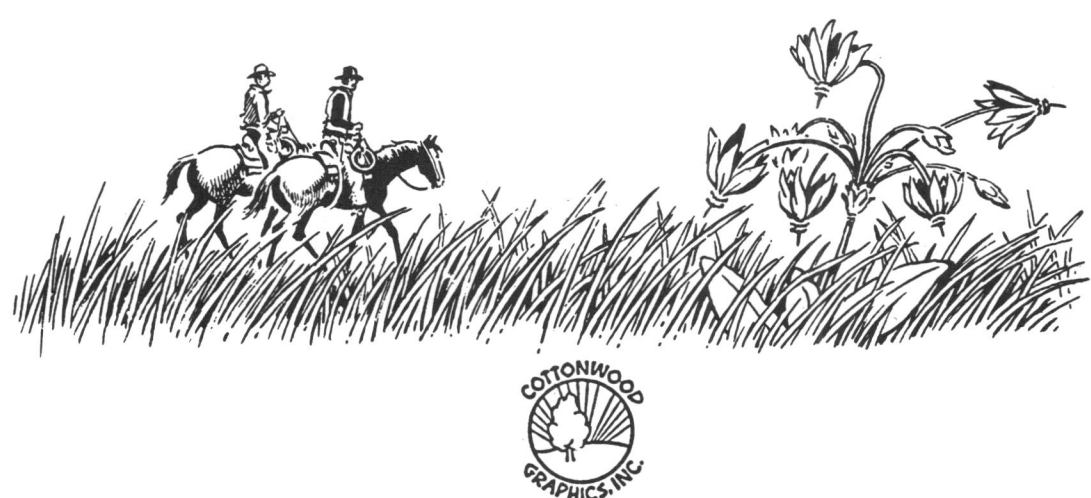

Other books by Stan Lynde

A Month of Sundays - The Best of Rick O'Shay and Hipshot

Rick O'Shay, Hipshot, and Me - A Memoir by Stan Lynde

Pardners, Book One: The Bonding

Pardners, Book Two: The Legacy

Latigo, Book One: 1979-1980

Latigo, Book Two: 1980-1981

The New Adventures of Rick O'Shay and Hipshot

The Price of Fame, Book One

The Price of Fame Book Two

*For a complete listing of Stan Lynde books, prints, and products, ask for **free** catalog, available from :*

Cottonwood Graphics
2340 Trumble Creek Road
Kalispell, MT 59901-6713

GRASS ROOTS

BY STAN LYNDE

COTTONWOOD GRAPHICS, INC.

COTTONWOOD PUBLISHING, INC.
Stan Lynde's Old West
2707 Hwy. 93 S.
Kalispell, MT 59901
800-937-6343

GRASS ROOTS by Stan Lynde

Published by Cottonwood Graphics, Inc.,
2340 Trumble Creek Road
Kalispell, Montana 59901-6713

GRASS ROOTS cartoons © 1984, 1985, 1993
by Stan Lynde

Editorial narrative © 1985, 1993 Stan Lynde

All rights reserved. No part of this book may be
reproduced or transmitted in any form or by any
means--except by a reviewer who may quote
brief passages in a review to be printed in
a magazine or newspaper--without permission in
writing from the publisher. For information, contact

Cottonwood Graphics, Inc.,
2340 Trumble Creek Road
Kalispell, MT 59901-6713

Printed in U.S.A.

35798642

Library of Congress Catalog Card Number: 91-077329

ISBN: 0-9626999-4-2

*To all the hard-working, honest, and courageous men, women, and children who **are** the Grass Roots of Montana, and America.*

VI.

Introduction

GRASS ROOTS first came into being in the fall of 1984 at the urging, and with the generous help and support, of fellow cartoonist Barry McWilliams, creator of the *J.P. DOODLES* cartoon.

It has long been my belief that the national media, for a variety of reasons, rarely reflects the views and values of the people in "grass roots" America, and my cartoon series was designed from the outset to try to do just that. Through my characters, *Billy* and *Shag*, I set out to express the feelings and attitudes of the people who are the very heart of America--people who are honest, hard-working, and patriotic, and who conduct their lives with courage, faith, and integrity.

These are the people who seldom make the headlines, people who work, save, raise their children, and pay their taxes. You'll find them in their homes, in their schools, on their jobs, at their places of worship, and in the voting booths during elections.

Their names reflect the nationalities, races, and creeds whose strengths have made America great, names which in many cases appear in the newspaper only at their births, their weddings, and their deaths.

They are patient, optimistic, long-suffering, and infinitely wise.

I like them.

A major goal of my work has always been to act as their spokesman, to express through humor the opinions and beliefs they hold, because I believe those opinions and beliefs are not only valid, but the very reason for our progress and success as a nation.

In the following pages you'll find cartoons on a variety of subjects--inflation, gun control, agriculture, victims' rights, child abuse, religion, politics, pride, and yes, prejudice. It is my hope that you'll find at least some of your ideas expressed, and that you'll be entertained.

If these cartoons bring you a smile or two of amusement and recognition, I'll consider this book a success.

Stan Lynde

Kalispell, Montana

I've always loved mountains. They give me peace, and a feeling of being close to God. And the more the world becomes settled, improved, and diminished by "progress" the more that love grows.

Comedian Gene Shepherd says he knows where the world is headed--"every square inch of its surface...*paved.*"

Well, I think he's wrong; there will always be mountains--high, free, and unimproved.

Thank God.

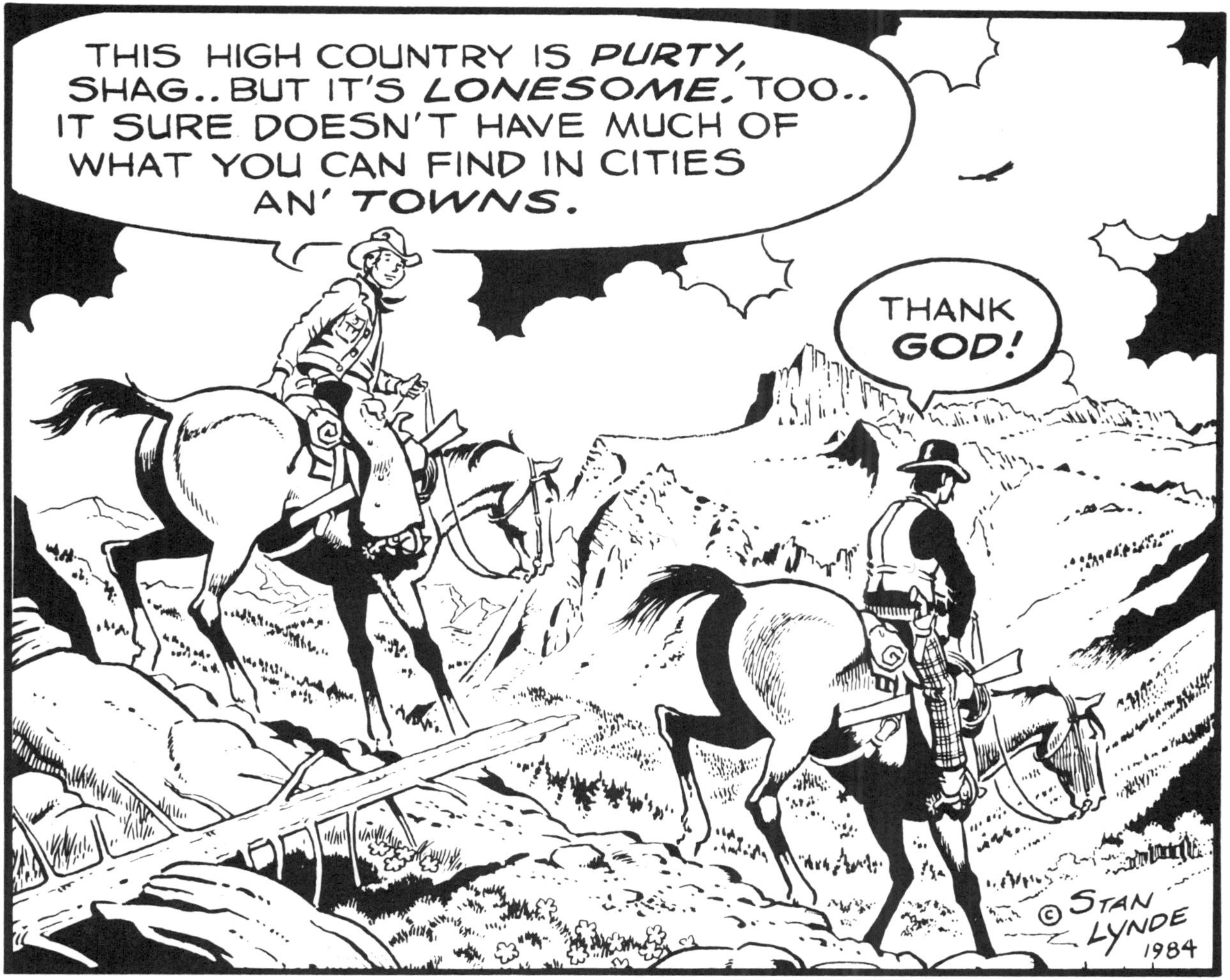
THIS HIGH COUNTRY IS PURTY, SHAG..BUT IT'S LONESOME, TOO.. IT SURE DOESN'T HAVE MUCH OF WHAT YOU CAN FIND IN CITIES AN' TOWNS.
THANK GOD!
© STAN LYNDE 1984

Cowboys traditionally work hard and play hard, and in the west the bar and saloon has always been the location for much of the play.

After a few belts of the local brave-maker, errors in judgment become the norm, and many a bow-legged puncher has found himself, like Shag, mixing it up with a few "playmates."

Cowboys call that "fun."

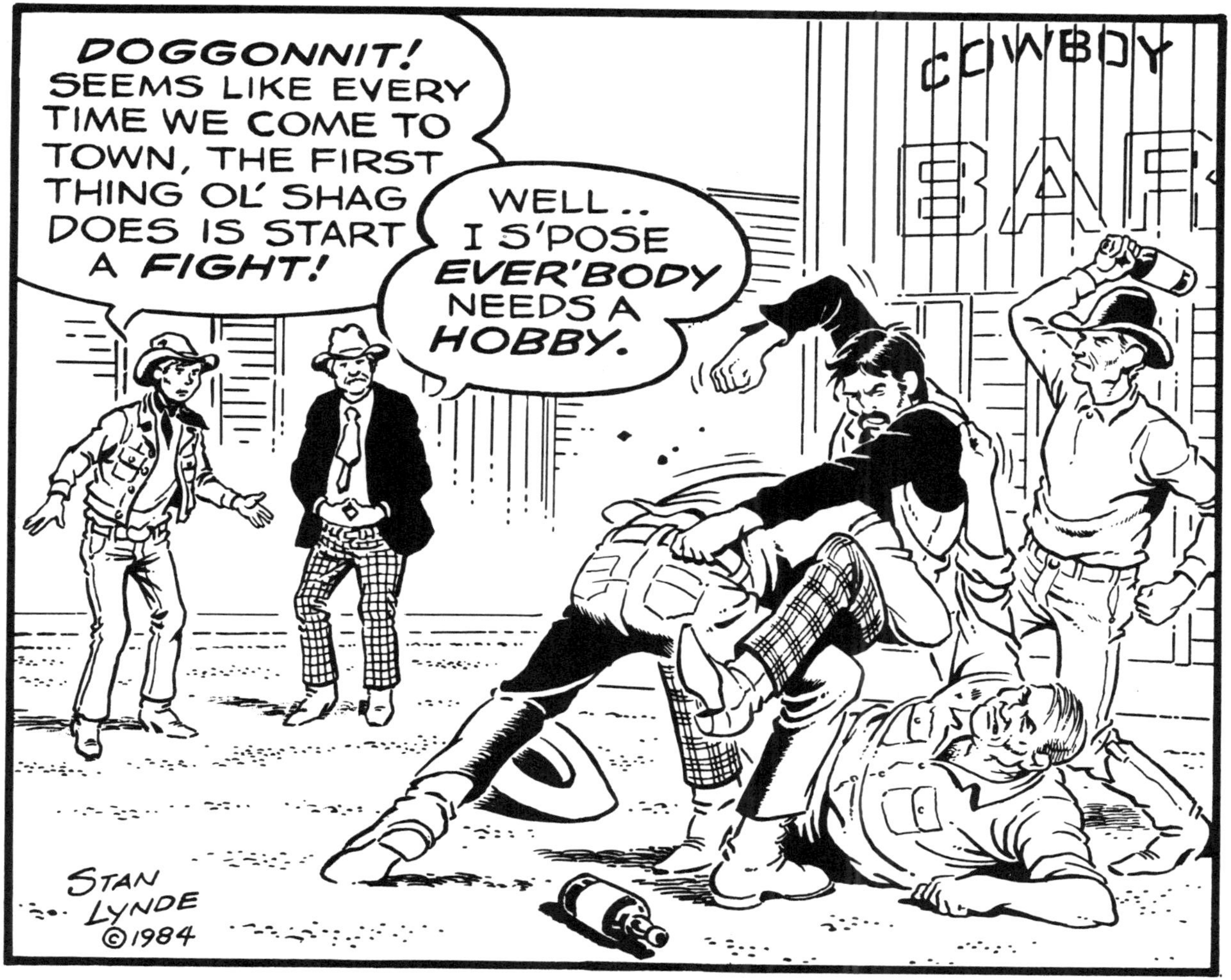
DOGGONNIT! SEEMS LIKE EVERY TIME WE COME TO TOWN, THE FIRST THING OL' SHAG DOES IS START A FIGHT!
WELL.. I S'POSE EVER'BODY NEEDS A HOBBY.
COWBOY BAR
STAN LYNDE ©1984

The idea for this cartoon was given me by my friend George Anderson. With his brother Dom, George owns and runs a service station where you can still get service.

Like most small-town businessmen, he's seen his share of good times and bad times.

George prefers the *good* times.

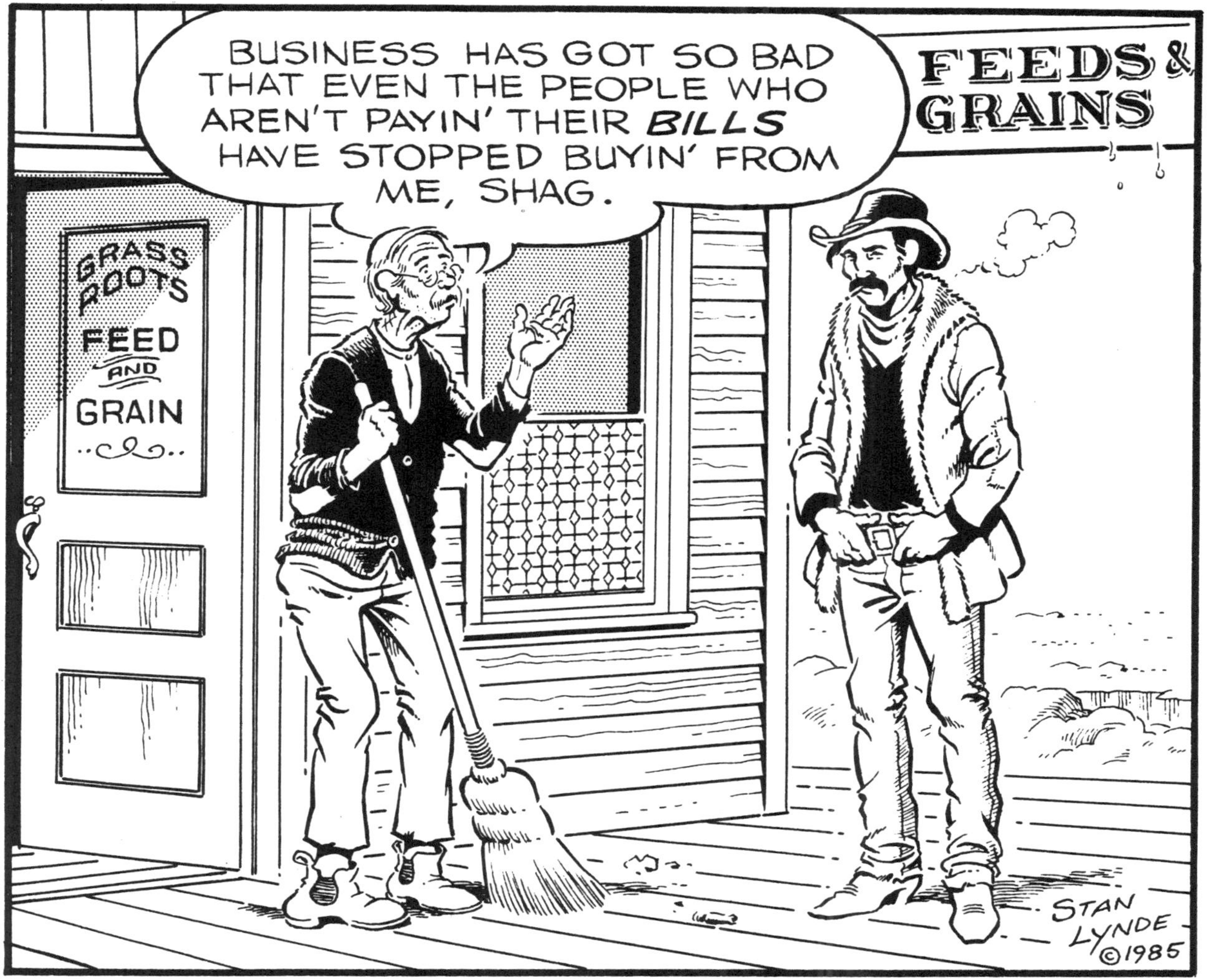
BUSINESS HAS GOT SO BAD THAT EVEN THE PEOPLE WHO AREN'T PAYIN' THEIR *BILLS* HAVE STOPPED BUYIN' FROM ME, SHAG.
FEEDS & GRAINS
GRASS ROOTS FEED AND GRAIN
STAN LYNDE ©1985

Like most cattlemen, the Major has a tough time feeling the bank really shares in the ownership of his cattle, even though he depends on borrowed money to operate.

After all, the banker doesn't ride a hay sled in winter, chop ice out of waterholes, brand calves, or ride bog, so the Major figures he deserves the lion's share of the partnership.

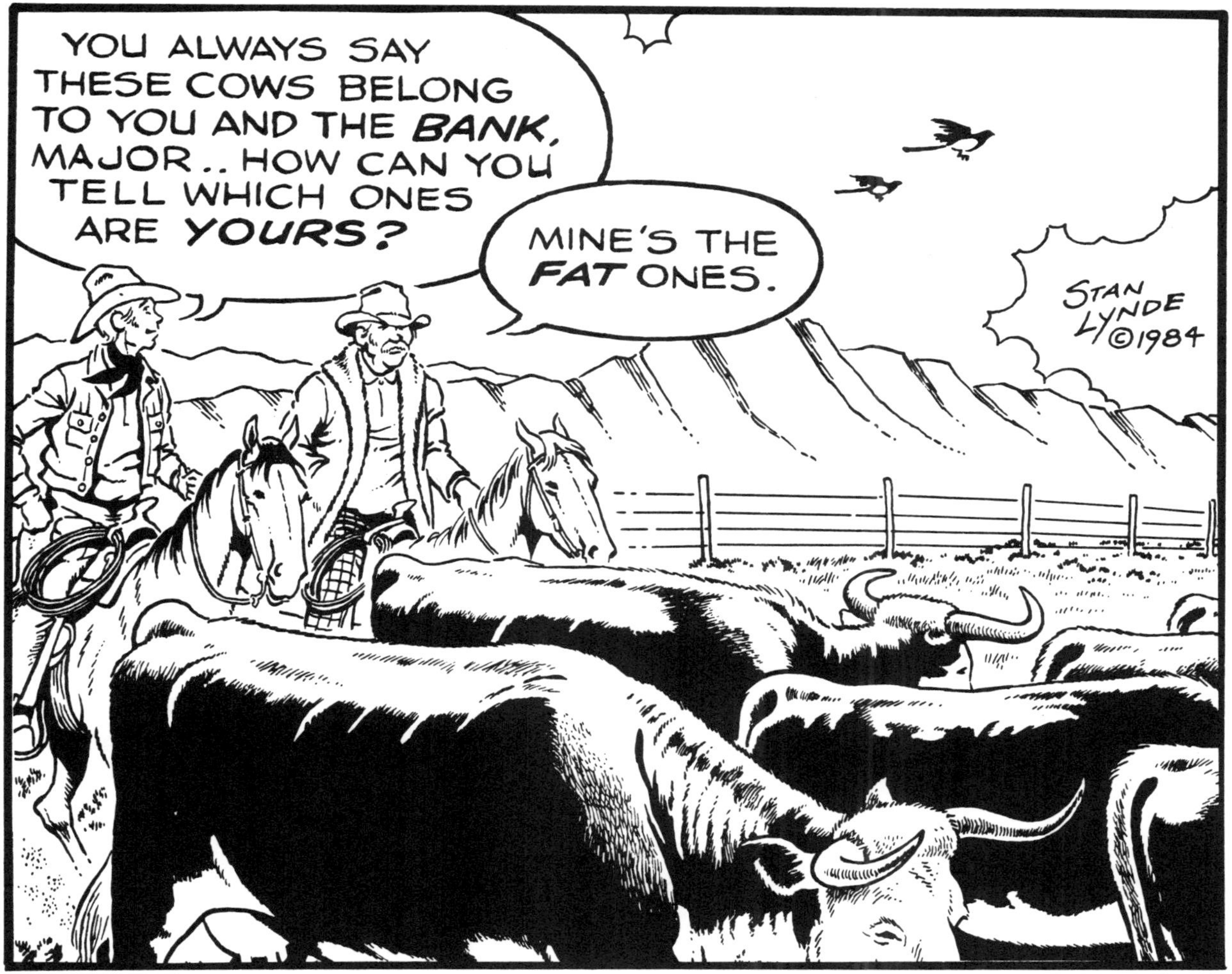
YOU ALWAYS SAY THESE COWS BELONG TO YOU AND THE BANK, MAJOR.. HOW CAN YOU TELL WHICH ONES ARE YOURS?
MINE'S THE FAT ONES.
STAN LYNDE ©1984

Kids *do* love cowboys; it seems to be some kind of universal truth.

Maybe it's the horses cowboys ride, or the free, natural life they follow, but the relationship between cowpunchers and youngsters is a special one on both sides.

Maybe it's just that in a very special way cowboys never really grow up.

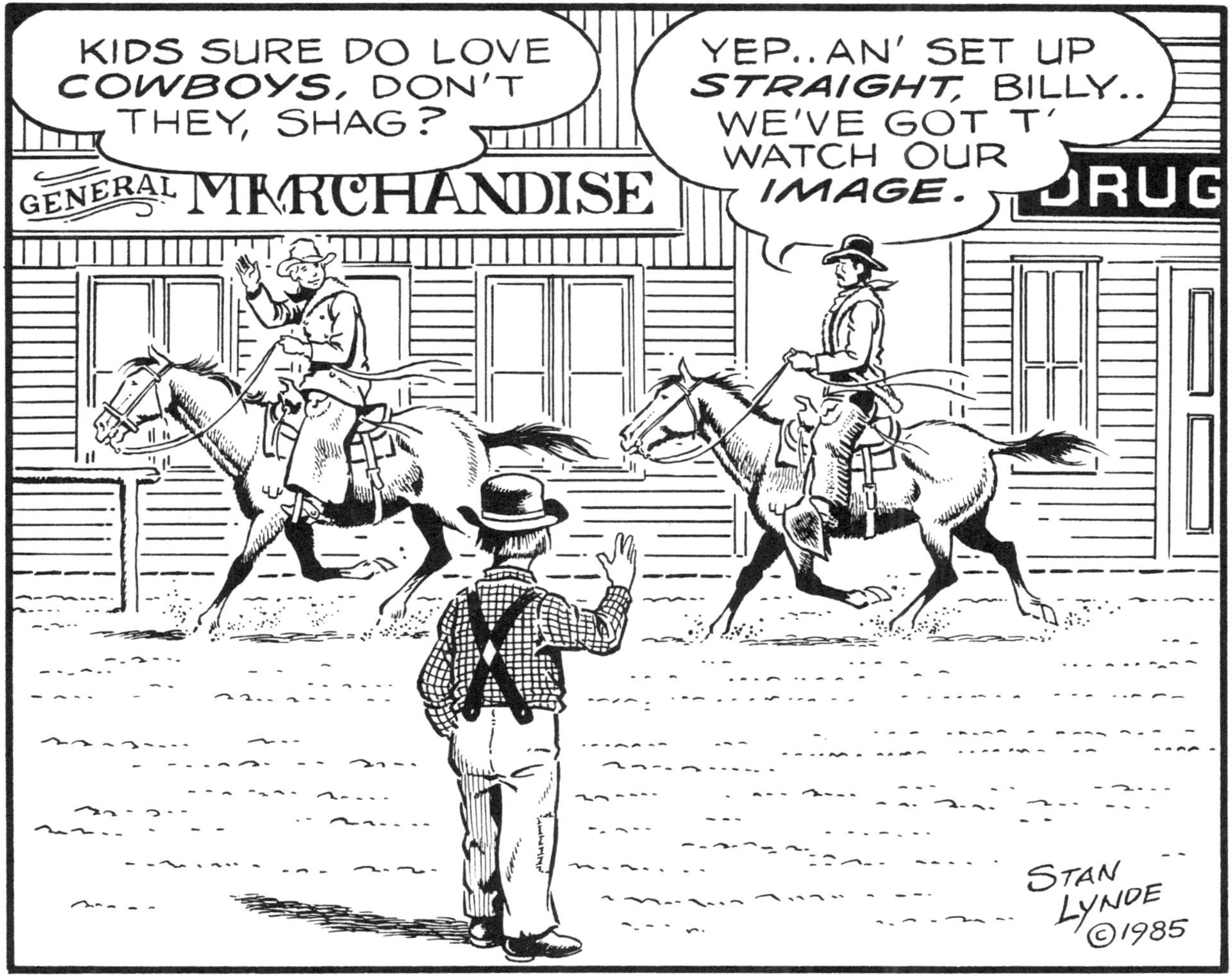
KIDS SURE DO LOVE COWBOYS, DON'T THEY, SHAG?
YEP..AN' SET UP STRAIGHT, BILLY.. WE'VE GOT T' WATCH OUR IMAGE.
GENERAL MERCHANDISE
DRUG
STAN LYNDE ©1985

These days the western boot is worn by people in nearly all walks of life and in all parts of the country, on city streets, in air-conditioned offices, at backyard barbecues, and cocktail parties.

Their footwear comes in lizard, snake, water buffalo, and ostrich, in colors and styles never dreamed of by the old-time cowboy, for whom boots were simply an important tool of his trade.

To the man who lived his life on horseback, boots were for riding.

Shoes were for walking.

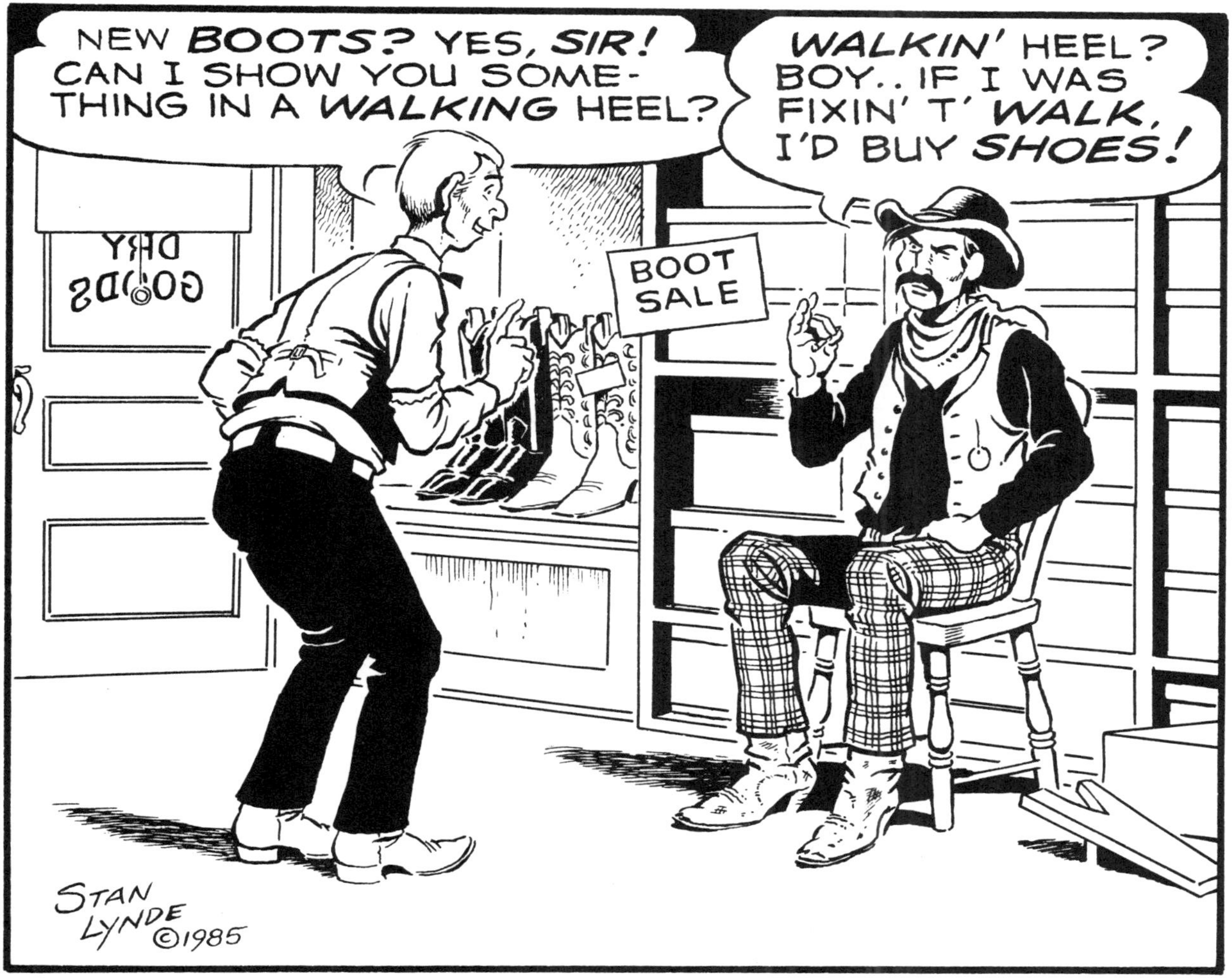
NEW BOOTS? YES, SIR! CAN I SHOW YOU SOME-THING IN A WALKING HEEL?
WALKIN' HEEL? BOY.. IF I WAS FIXIN' T' WALK, I'D BUY SHOES!
BOOT SALE
STAN LYNDE ©1985

I love horses. They're big, strong, loyal animals--with little *teeny* brains.

Ideally, their riders should calm their fears and control them, preferably by being at least *slightly* more intelligent.

There are times, though, when friend horse makes his own independent decisions, and they seldom agree with what the rider has in mind.

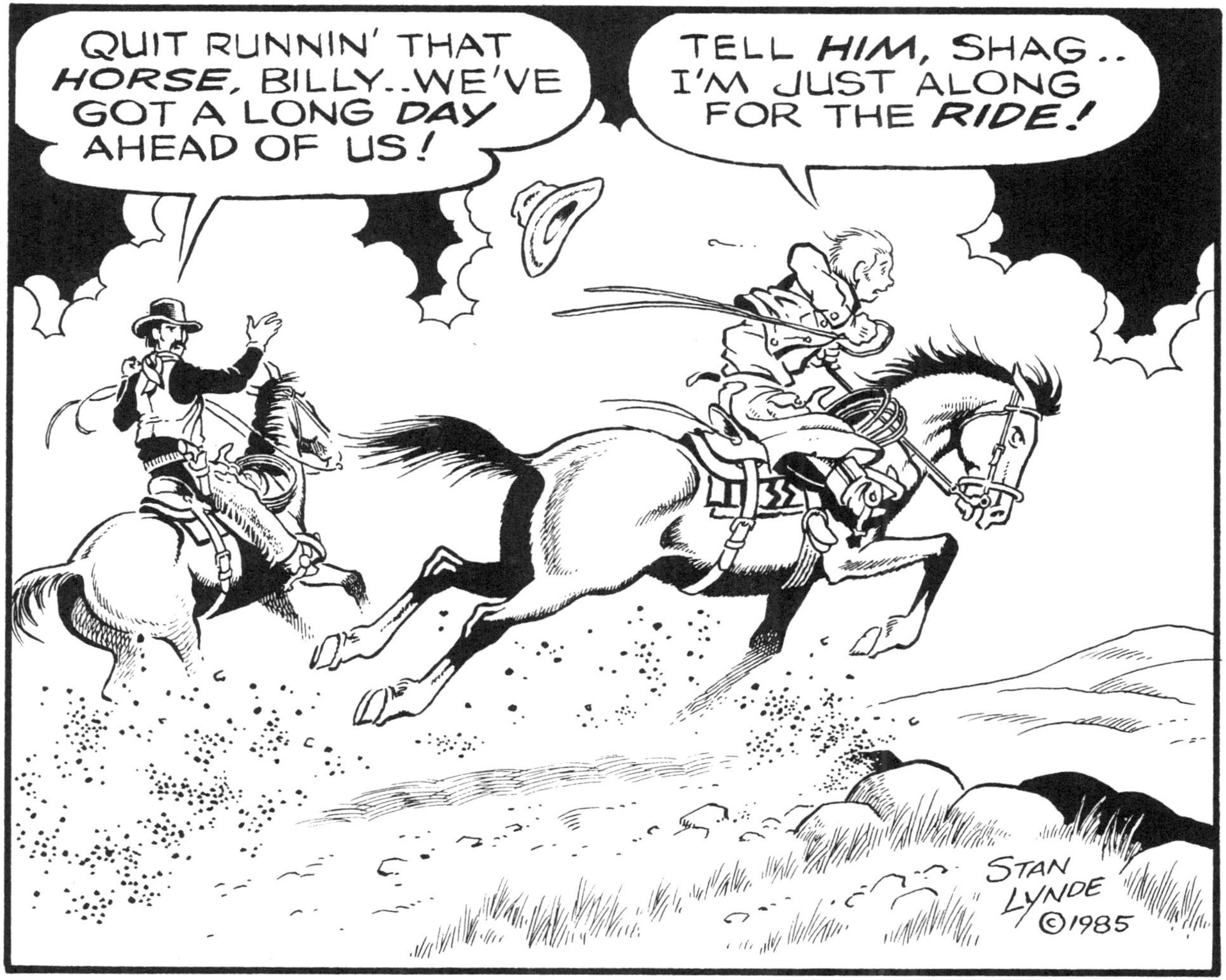
QUIT RUNNIN' THAT HORSE, BILLY..WE'VE GOT A LONG DAY AHEAD OF US!
TELL HIM, SHAG.. I'M JUST ALONG FOR THE RIDE!
STAN LYNDE ©1985

Shag has apparently been misled sometime in the past by appearances, enough to develop a degree of caution, at least. Billy, on the other hand, remains an eternal optimist.

He knows that everything that glitters isn't *gold,* but he knows, too, that gold certainly does *glitter*.

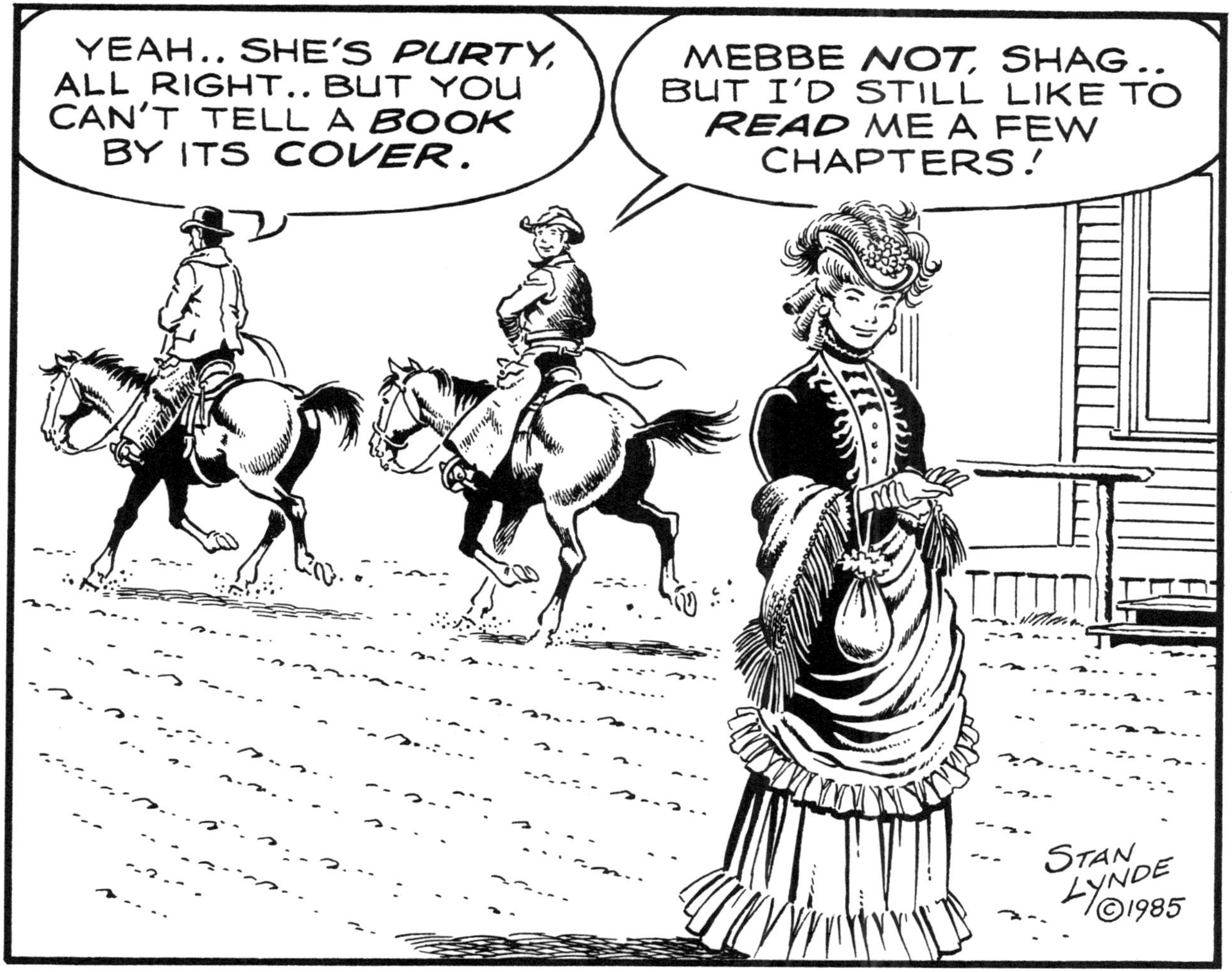
YEAH.. SHE'S PURTY, ALL RIGHT.. BUT YOU CAN'T TELL A BOOK BY ITS COVER.
MEBBE NOT, SHAG.. BUT I'D STILL LIKE TO READ ME A FEW CHAPTERS!
STAN LYNDE ©1985

As a Christian, I've learned that the meaning of Easter is indeed new life.

Beyond the mystery of the resurrection to new and eternal life is the remarkable fact that belief in the Easter story leads to new life in the *now*.

The preachers call that "gospel", a word that means "good news."

I can't think of any *better* news.

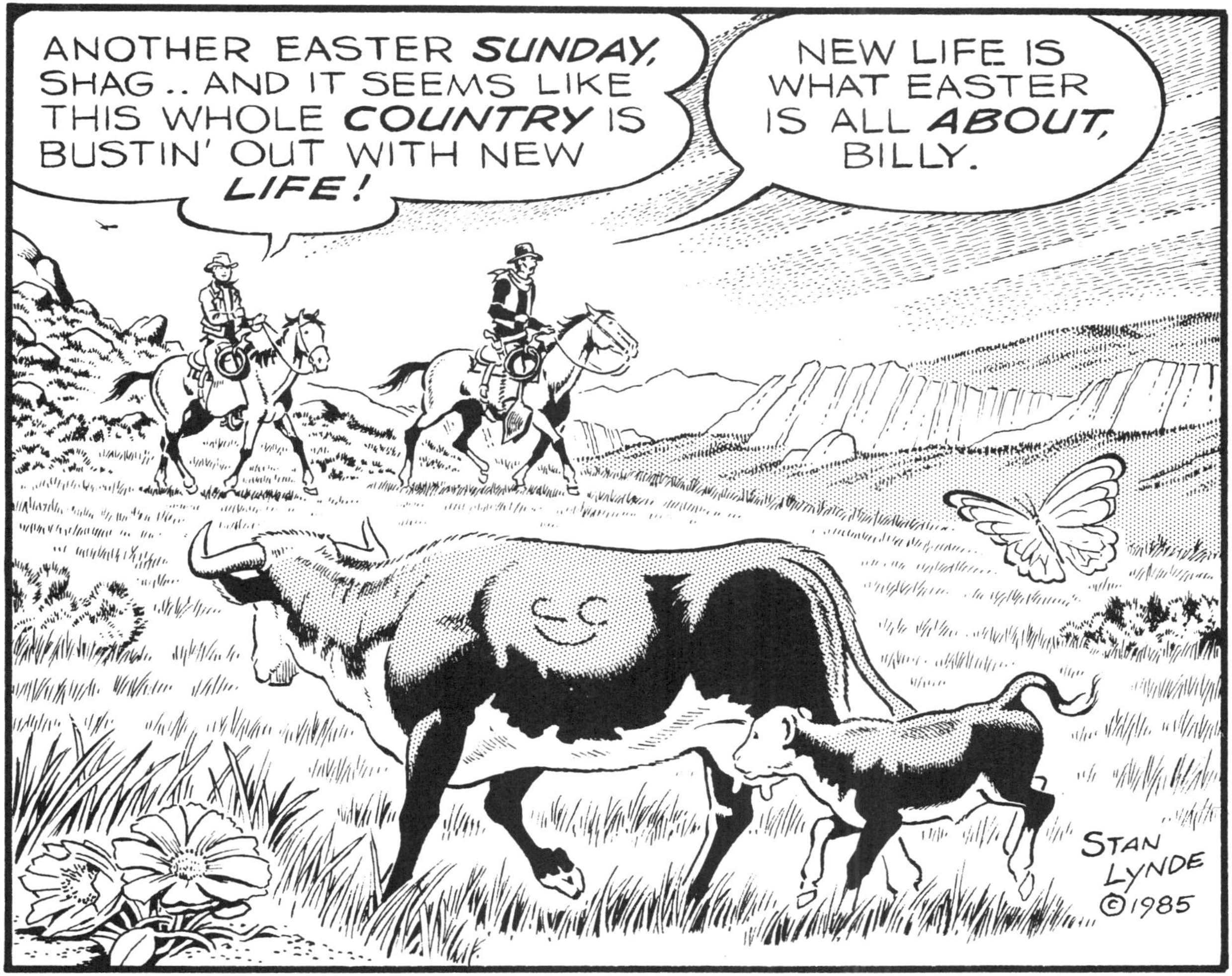
ANOTHER EASTER SUNDAY, SHAG .. AND IT SEEMS LIKE THIS WHOLE COUNTRY IS BUSTIN' OUT WITH NEW LIFE!
NEW LIFE IS WHAT EASTER IS ALL ABOUT, BILLY.
STAN LYNDE ©1985

It's hard for most people in the west to believe that because guns are used by criminals to commit crimes the ownership and use of firearms by responsible, law-abiding people should be restricted or denied.

It's hard for *me* to believe it, too.

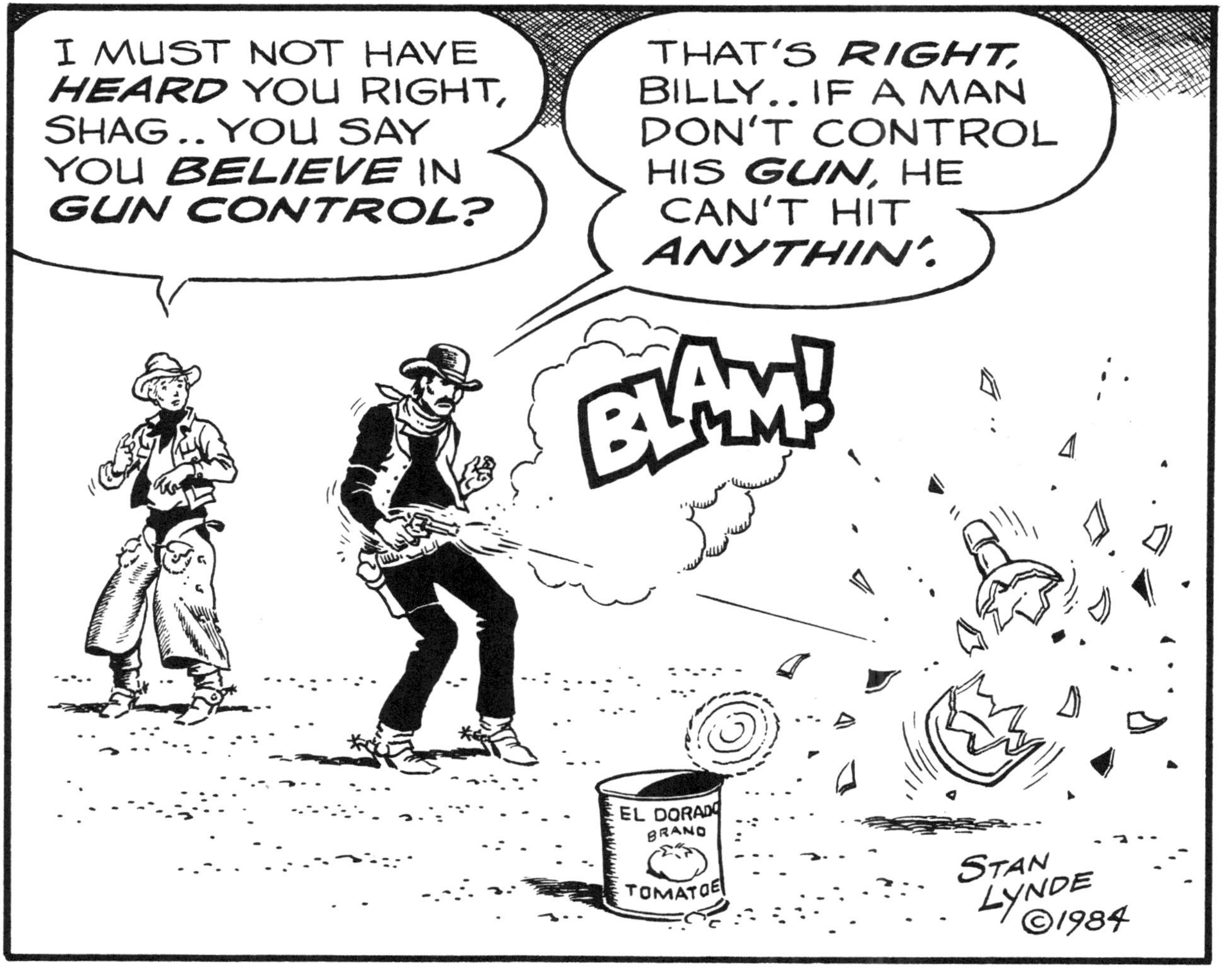
I MUST NOT HAVE HEARD YOU RIGHT, SHAG.. YOU SAY YOU BELIEVE IN GUN CONTROL?
THAT'S RIGHT, BILLY.. IF A MAN DON'T CONTROL HIS GUN, HE CAN'T HIT ANYTHIN'.
BLAM!
EL DORADO BRAND TOMATOE
STAN LYNDE ©1984

"Nothing ventured, nothing gained" seems to be Billy's motto, but he's about to learn that where there's a possibility of gain there's also the possibility of loss--such as a *tooth* or two.

Shag isn't likely to provide physical help to his pardner during the upcoming conflict, but he'll certainly be on hand to pick him up when it's over.

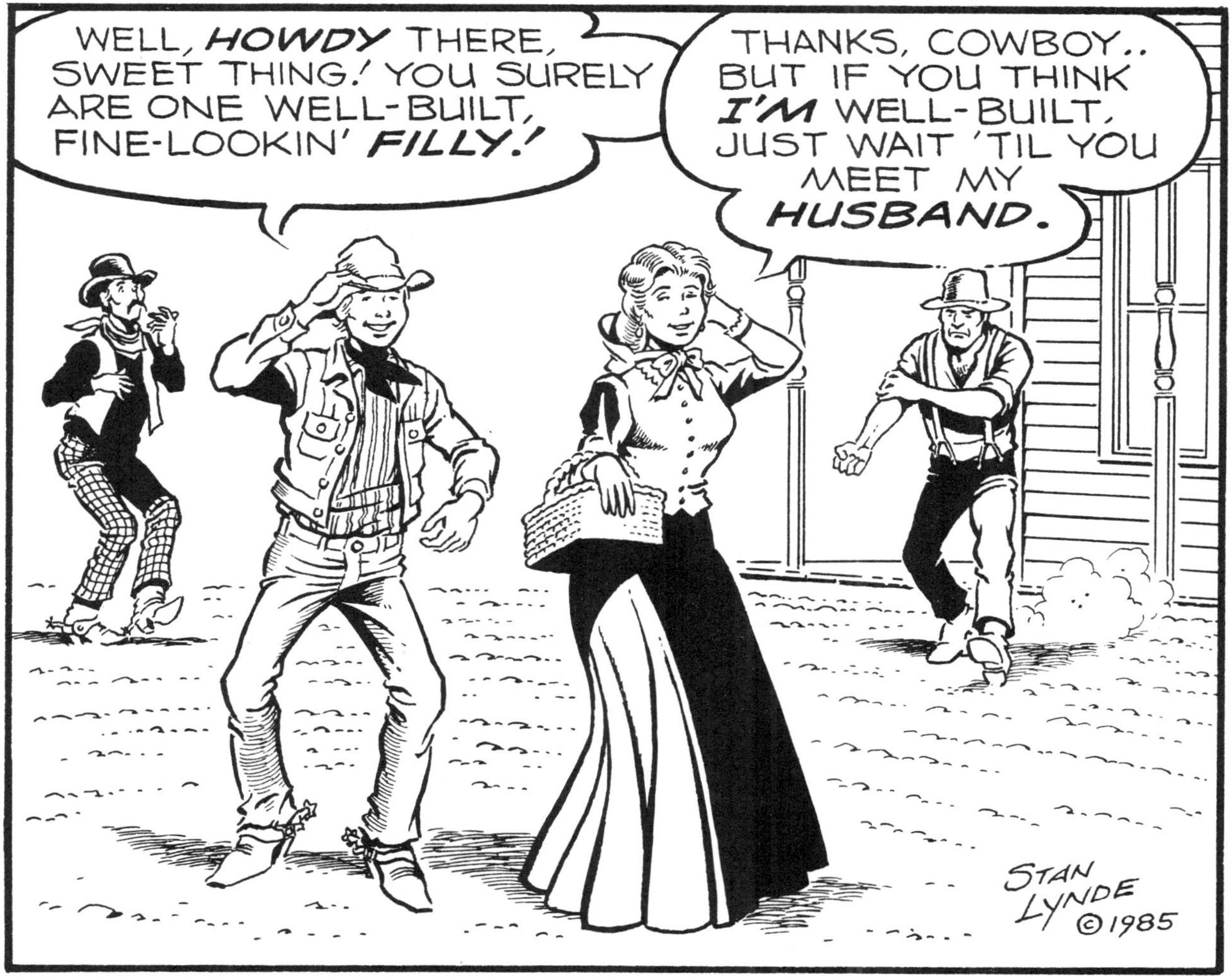
WELL, **HOWDY** THERE, SWEET THING! YOU SURELY ARE ONE WELL-BUILT, FINE-LOOKIN' **FILLY!**
THANKS, COWBOY.. BUT IF YOU THINK **I'M** WELL-BUILT, JUST WAIT 'TIL YOU MEET MY **HUSBAND.**
STAN LYNDE ©1985

Hindsight, it is said, is always 20-20, but the trouble with hindsight is that it always comes too late to be of any real help.

Ranching may not be, as some cynics have said, the triumph of hope over experience, but it is true that the outcome for the rancher is never certain.

For many a cowman, the *good* year is always *next* year.

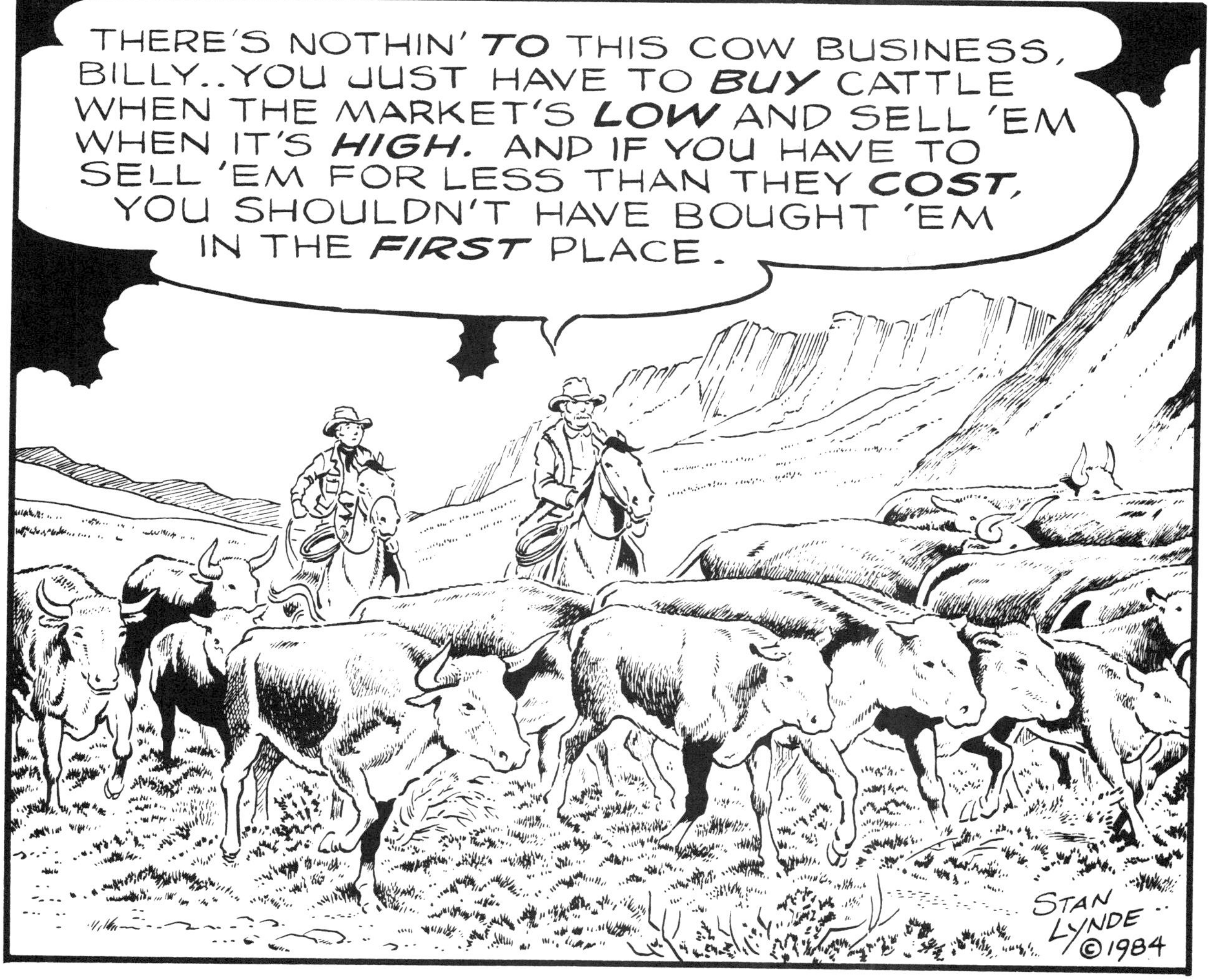
THERE'S NOTHIN' TO THIS COW BUSINESS, BILLY..YOU JUST HAVE TO BUY CATTLE WHEN THE MARKET'S LOW AND SELL 'EM WHEN IT'S HIGH. AND IF YOU HAVE TO SELL 'EM FOR LESS THAN THEY COST, YOU SHOULDN'T HAVE BOUGHT 'EM IN THE FIRST PLACE.
STAN LYNDE ©1984

Inflation seems to be a permanent fact of life, no matter what the economists tell us.

I had an economics professor in college who spent most of one quarter teaching us that if a man wanted *two* things, but had money for only *one,* he'd buy the one he wanted *most.*

I never *did* understand economics.

In this cartoon, Shag has been struck by the latest postal increase and, being a practical man, has sought outside financing in order to keep up with his correspondence.

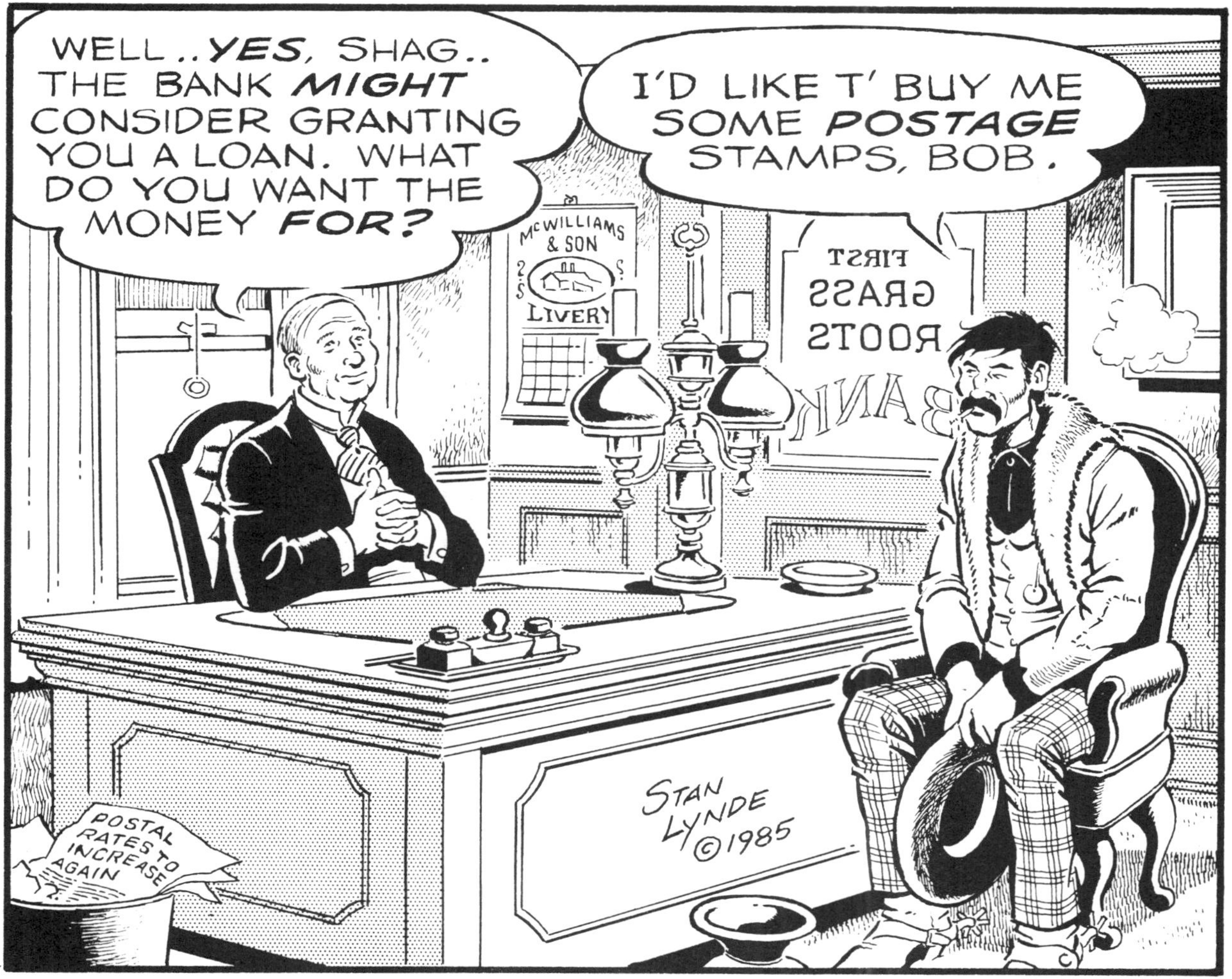
WELL ..YES, SHAG.. THE BANK MIGHT CONSIDER GRANTING YOU A LOAN. WHAT DO YOU WANT THE MONEY FOR?
I'D LIKE T' BUY ME SOME POSTAGE STAMPS, BOB.
McWILLIAMS & SON LIVERY
FIRST GRASS ROOTS BANK
POSTAL RATES TO INCREASE AGAIN
STAN LYNDE ©1985

In such "primitive" societies as that of the American Indian old age is respected, admired, and utilized. The experience of a lifetime and the wisdom gained from it is considered an asset, not only to the individual but to society at large.

In modern cultures such as ours the accent is on youth--being young, looking young, and staying young. Not only are advanced age and its wisdom not valued, they are all too often ignored and denied.

Forced retirement and the warehousing of our older Americans is not only a disservice to them and to the contributions they can make, but to our advancement and progress as a nation, as well.

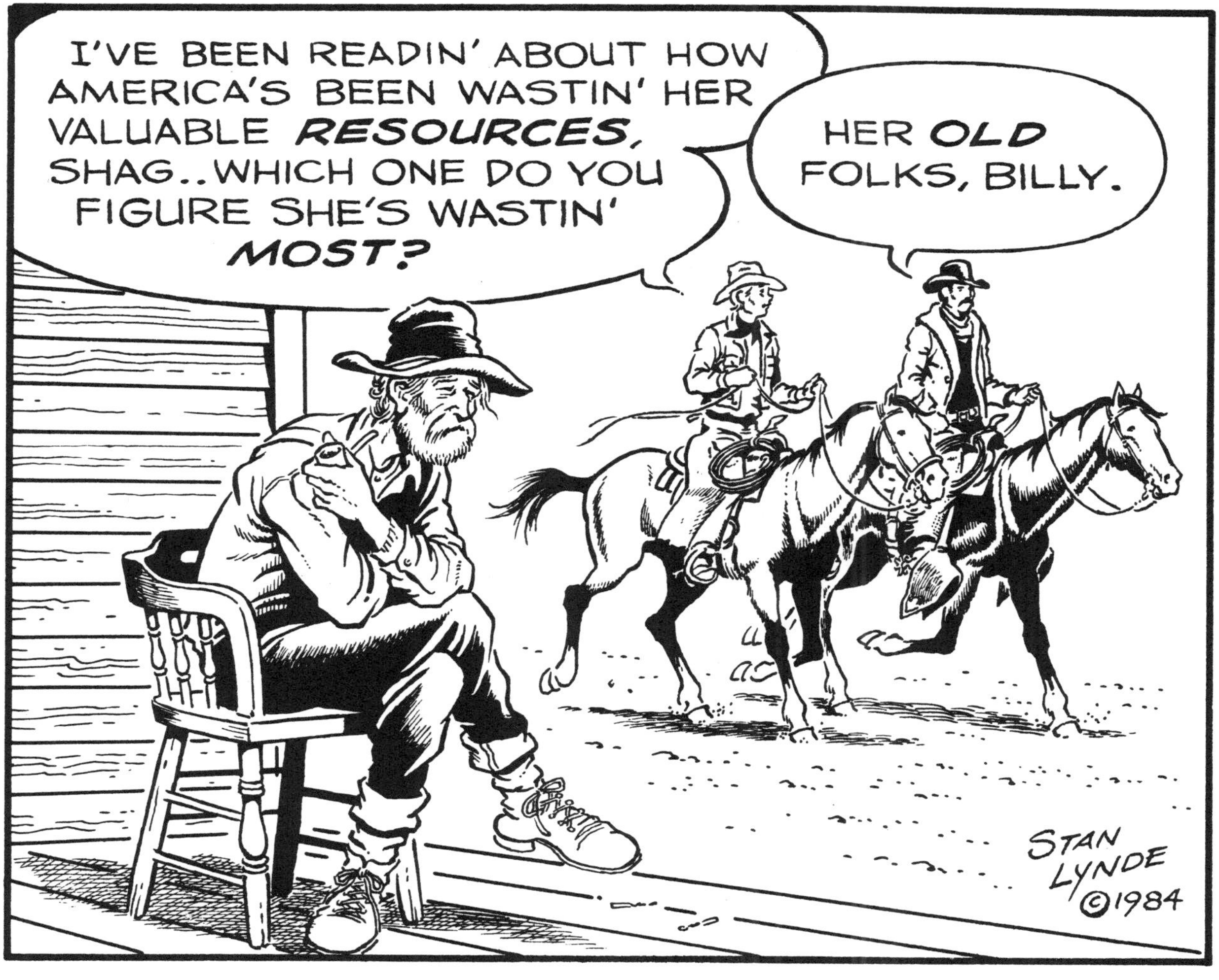
I'VE BEEN READIN' ABOUT HOW AMERICA'S BEEN WASTIN' HER VALUABLE RESOURCES, SHAG..WHICH ONE DO YOU FIGURE SHE'S WASTIN' MOST?
HER OLD FOLKS, BILLY.
STAN LYNDE ©1984

Cattle and the cattle business have changed over the years as cattlemen have sought to improve the breed and their methods of operation.

The average steer today has little contact with that special tool of the working cowboy, the *reata*, lariat, or rope, and in Shag's opinion just the *sight* of one by a modern beef critter is enough to cause him trauma and emotional upset.

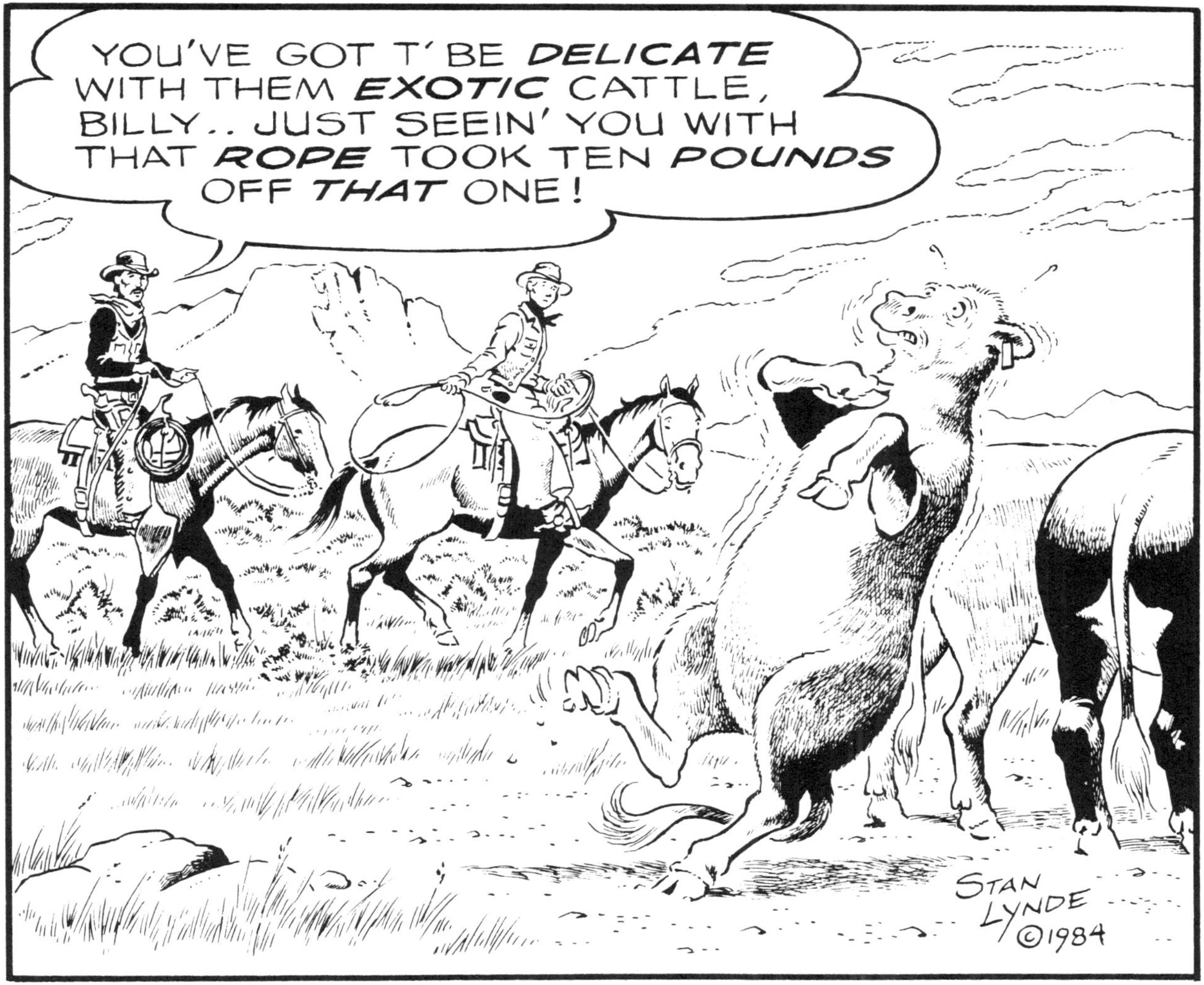
YOU'VE GOT T' BE ***DELICATE*** WITH THEM ***EXOTIC*** CATTLE, BILLY.. JUST SEEIN' YOU WITH THAT ***ROPE*** TOOK TEN ***POUNDS*** OFF ***THAT*** ONE!
STAN LYNDE ©1984

Perhaps it's true, as some have said, that it's only that more cases of child abuse are reported and identified today, but it does seem that children in these modern times are subject to more harm from adults than they used to be. Beatings, abandonment, sexual abuse, and the growing "kiddy porn" industry are a disgrace to the society in which they're committed.

However, I do think it's to our credit as a nation that the problem concerns us and that so many dedicated people are now committed to its reduction and elimination.

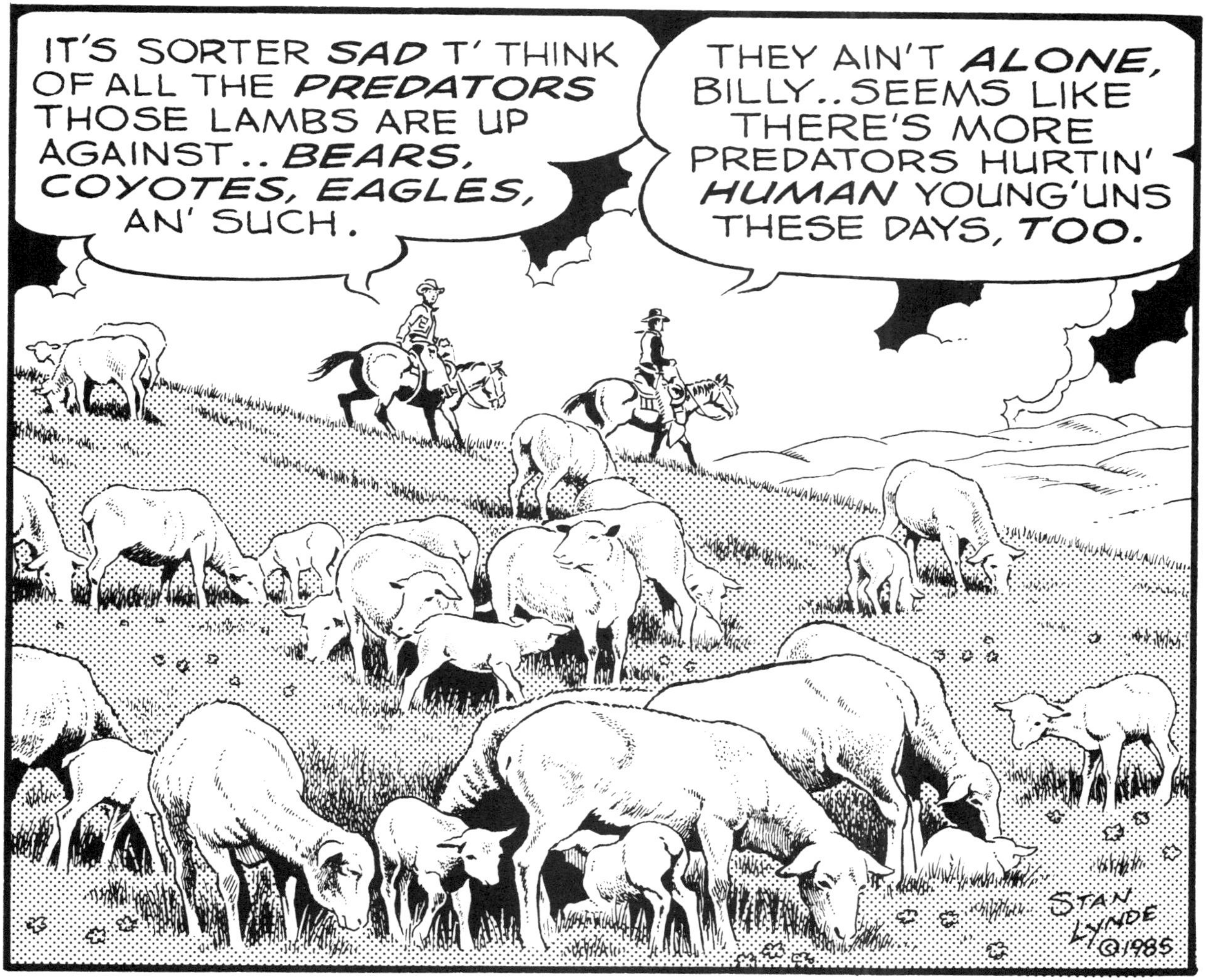
IT'S SORTER SAD T' THINK OF ALL THE PREDATORS THOSE LAMBS ARE UP AGAINST.. BEARS, COYOTES, EAGLES, AN' SUCH.
THEY AIN'T ALONE, BILLY..SEEMS LIKE THERE'S MORE PREDATORS HURTIN' HUMAN YOUNG'UNS THESE DAYS, TOO.
STAN LYNDE ©1985

When you tighten the cinch on a frosty morning, and your horse flattens his ears and humps up until a fair-size cat could make its home under your saddle skirts, you know your day's about to begin with a contest. And you know when it begins there's no way of predicting the directions and geographic locations that will be covered.

As for Shag, snug in his bedroll, there's no real need for him to worry. It's a rare horse who'll step on a man if he can help it.

Just the same, a half ton of horseflesh landing nearby with all four feet makes a *dandy* alarm clock.

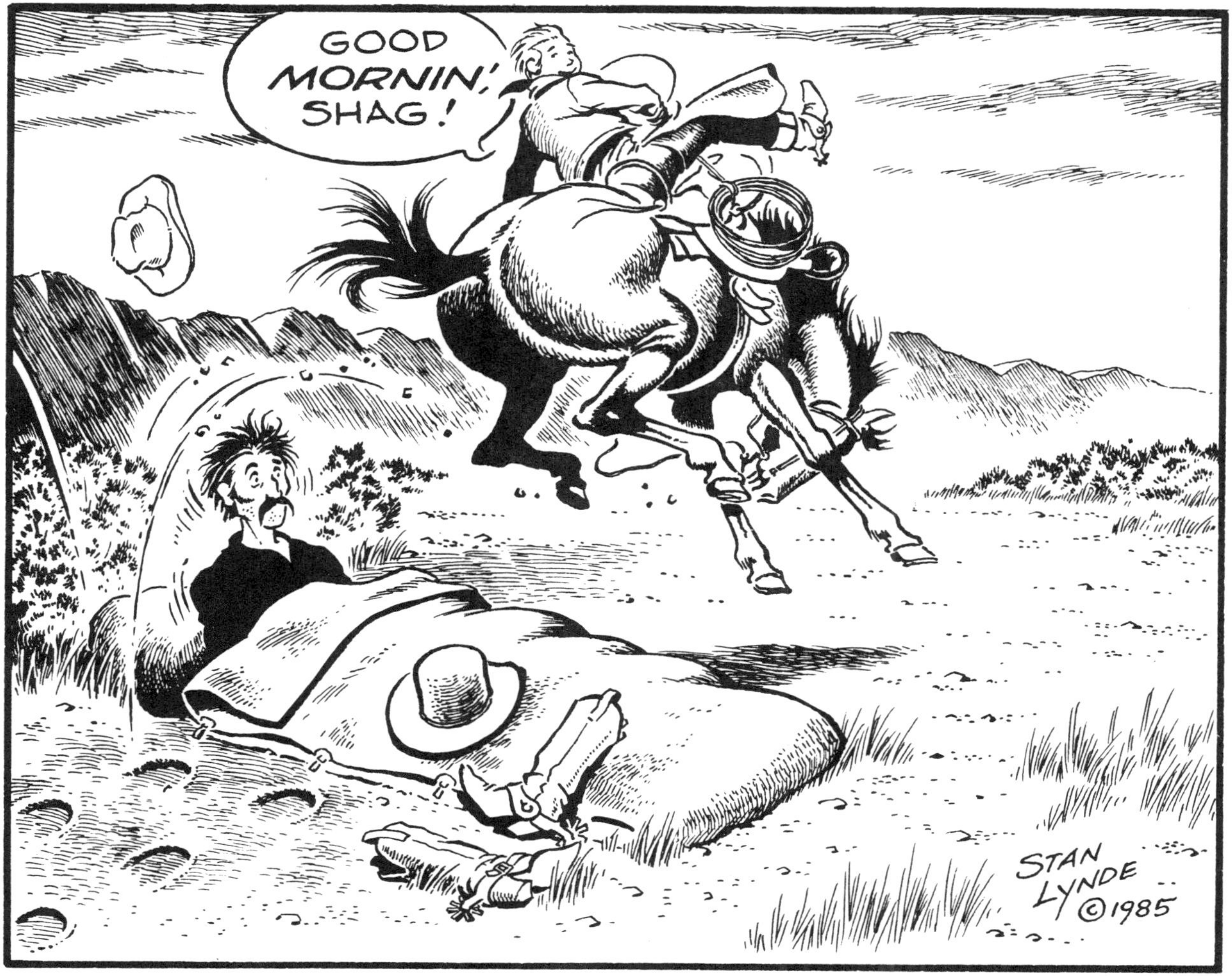
GOOD MORNIN', SHAG!
STAN LYNDE ©1985

Shag doesn't know much about kings; his ideas about men of power are limited to the ones *he* knows.

The office of county commissioner, in our western states, is a unique and important one. Of all elected officials the county commissioner is usually the most visible in the rural areas. He administers large amounts of public money and he oversees vast networks of rural roads, culverts, crossings, and bridges.

If he does his job well, or can at least create the impression that he does, he can parlay a string of six-year terms into a lifetime career.

Like other elected officials, his success depends not so much on how well he *does* the job as it does on how well his constituents *think* he does it, and sometimes a clever and dishonest man can remain in office for a long, long time.

Still, I believe Lincoln was right--you *can't* fool all of the people all of the time.

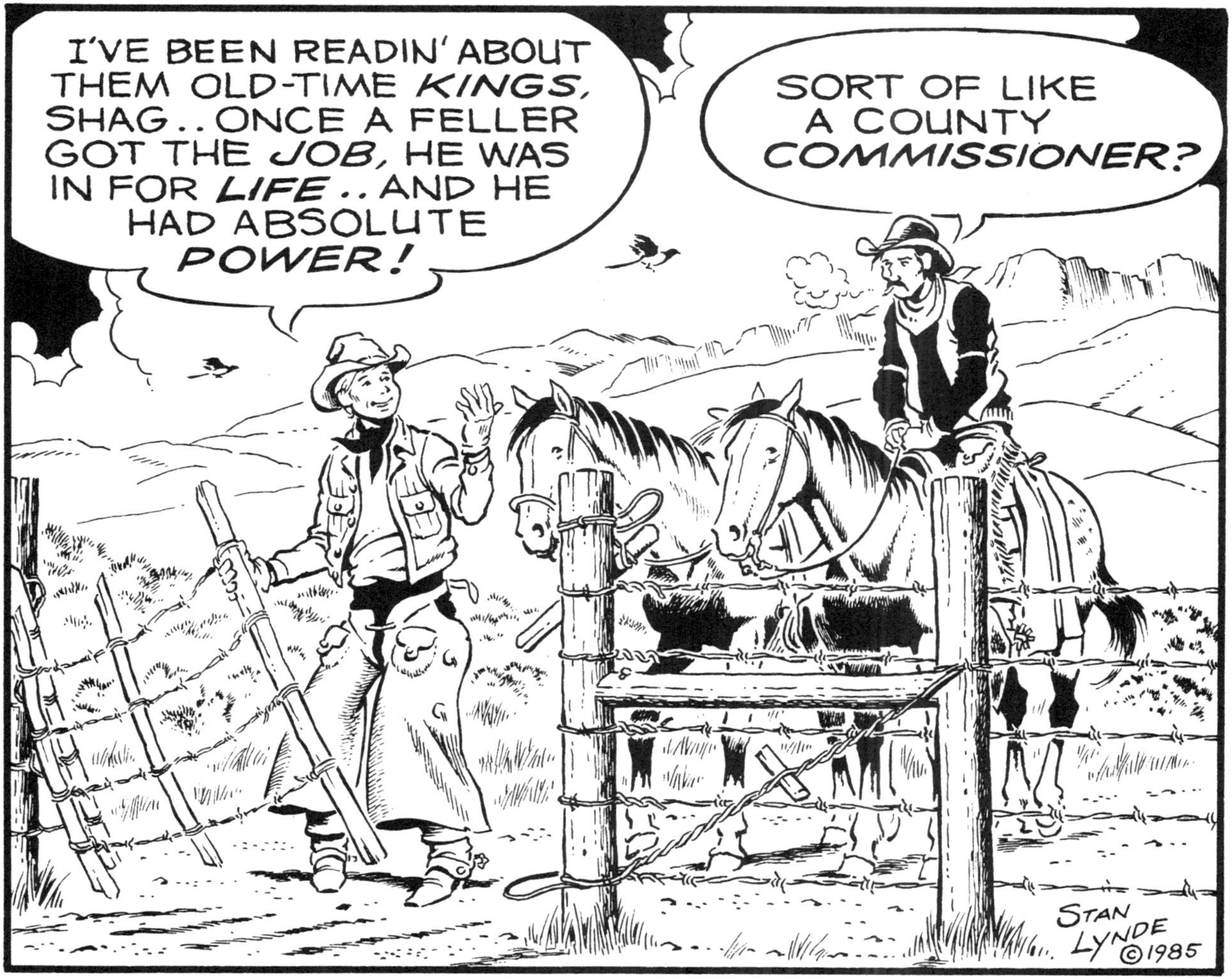
I'VE BEEN READIN' ABOUT THEM OLD-TIME KINGS, SHAG..ONCE A FELLER GOT THE JOB, HE WAS IN FOR LIFE..AND HE HAD ABSOLUTE POWER!
SORT OF LIKE A COUNTY COMMISSIONER?
STAN LYNDE ©1985

Our perceptions differ because each of us views the world from our own unique vantage point. Experience, wisdom, and a working knowledge of how things really are make for the best and most accurate observations.

And sometimes, as in this case, so does *elevation*.

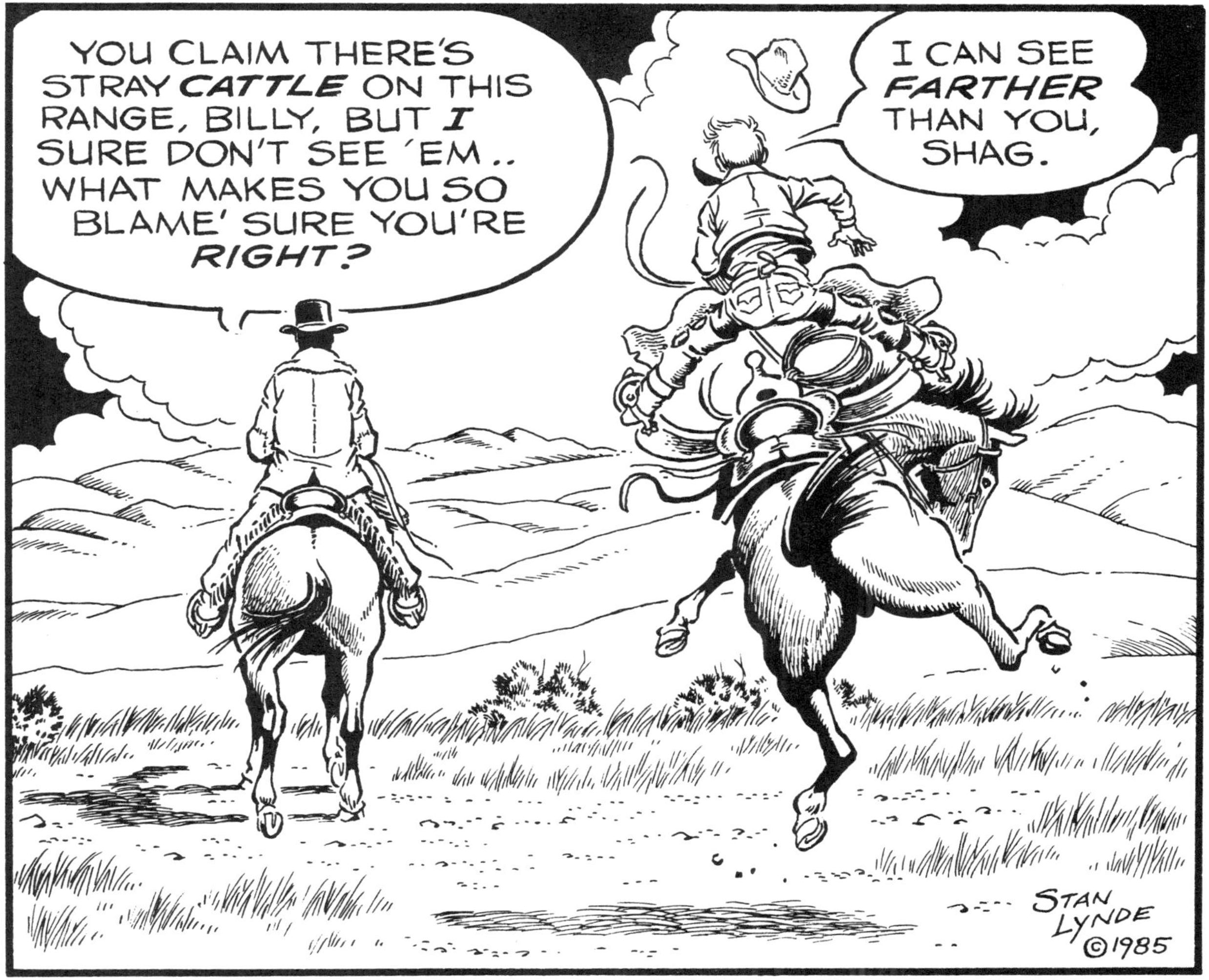
YOU CLAIM THERE'S STRAY CATTLE ON THIS RANGE, BILLY, BUT I SURE DON'T SEE 'EM.. WHAT MAKES YOU SO BLAME' SURE YOU'RE RIGHT?
I CAN SEE FARTHER THAN YOU, SHAG.
STAN LYNDE ©1985

Shag is not one to accept every statement he hears as truth; he tends to study a problem or situation until he feels he understands it and then form his own conclusion.

His perceptions may or may not be accurate, but like most of us once he's formed them they're accepted as true, regardless of facts or opinions to the contrary.

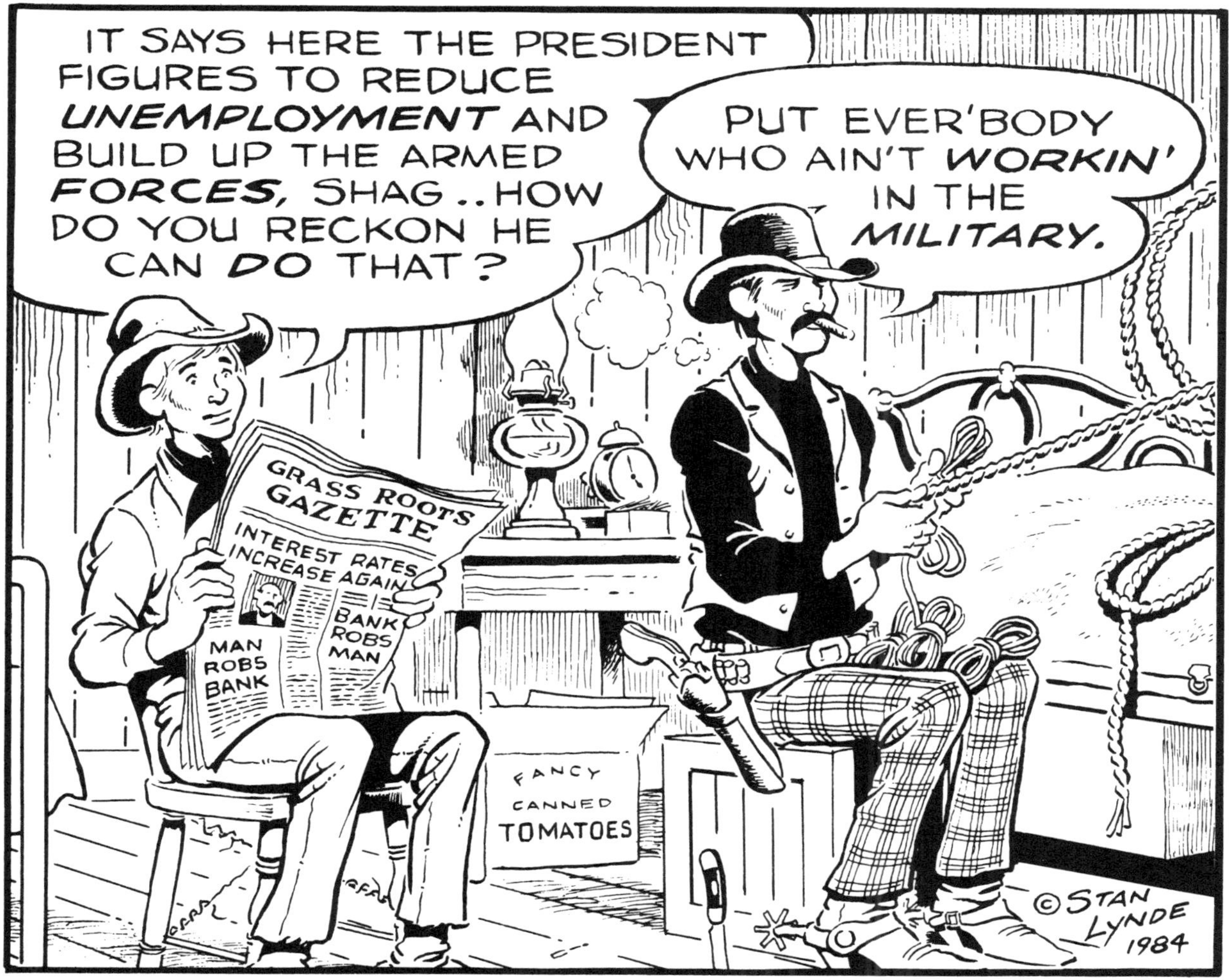
IT SAYS HERE THE PRESIDENT FIGURES TO REDUCE ***UNEMPLOYMENT*** AND BUILD UP THE ARMED ***FORCES,*** SHAG .. HOW DO YOU RECKON HE CAN ***DO*** THAT?
PUT EVER'BODY WHO AIN'T ***WORKIN'*** IN THE ***MILITARY.***
GRASS ROOTS GAZETTE
INTEREST RATES INCREASE AGAIN
MAN ROBS BANK
BANK ROBS MAN
FANCY CANNED TOMATOES
©STAN LYNDE 1984

If beauty is in the eye of the beholder, then so is reality. For each of us, at any given moment, reality is what we *perceive* it to be. If it's cold where we are, then it's cold; if it's raining where we are, then it's *raining*.

I read about a woman once who lived in Dodge City, Kansas during its wildest days. Now-famous gunmen like Wyatt Earp, Bat Masterson, and Doc Holliday fought other men in its streets and saloons. Texas cowboys drove wild-eyed longhorns up the long trail and through the streets, and those who knew Dodge well in those days describe it as the nearest thing to hell we're likely to find in this life.

But the woman lived there then, too, and she describes it as a good town with good people. Her life was spent living quietly, raising her children, attending church services, afternoon teas, and quilting bees.

Same town, different realities.

For Shag, it's *raining*.

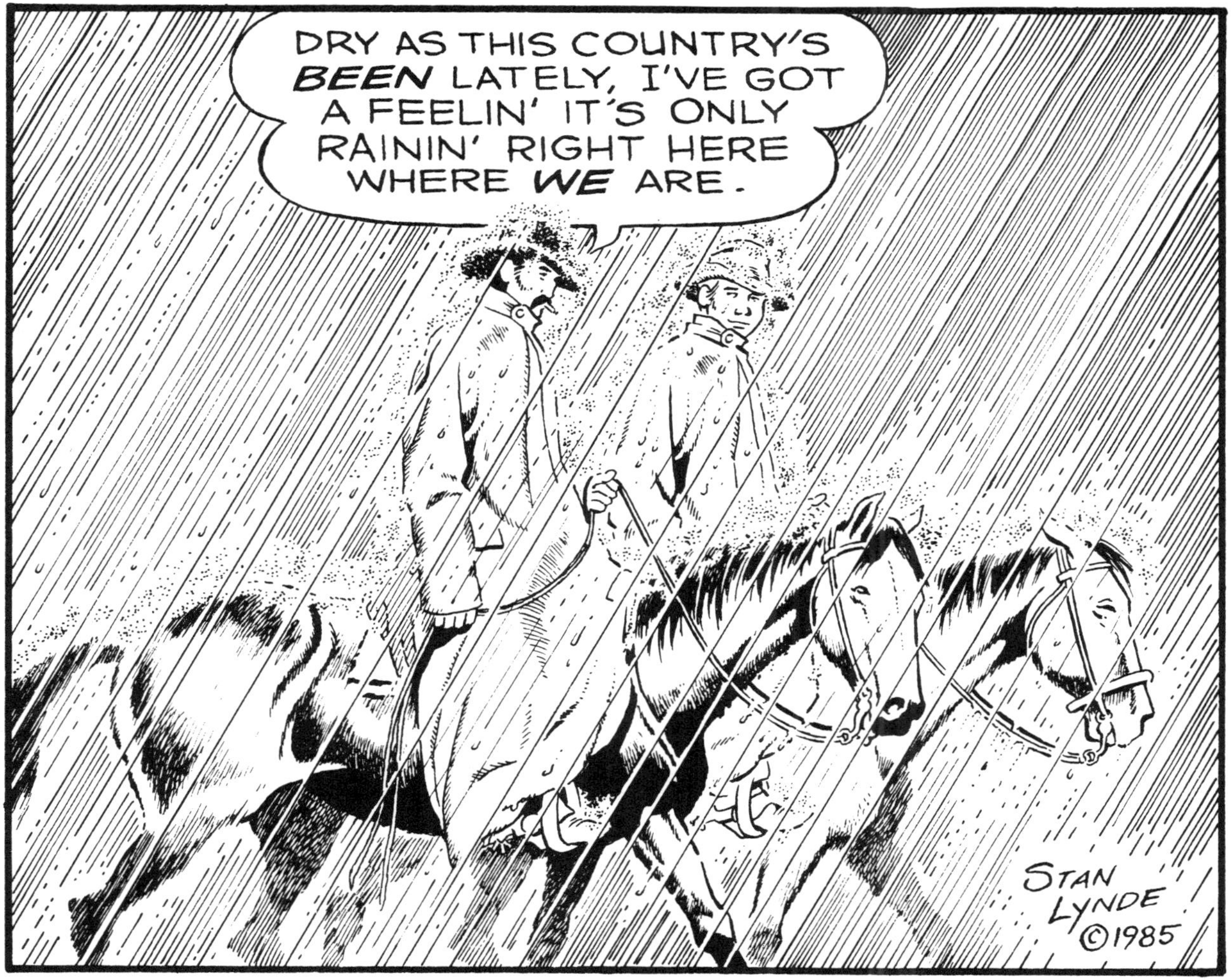
DRY AS THIS COUNTRY'S **BEEN** LATELY, I'VE GOT A FEELIN' IT'S ONLY RAININ' RIGHT HERE WHERE **WE** ARE.
STAN LYNDE ©1985

Nature's ecosystems are in a state of delicate balance that man, with his arrogance and technology, can easily damage and destroy. But endangered species are not limited to the spotted owl, condor, and trumpeter swan--even institutions can qualify.

To Shag, the family farm is such an endangered species, and threats to *its* existence may include inflation, land developers, foreign imports, and bureaucrats.

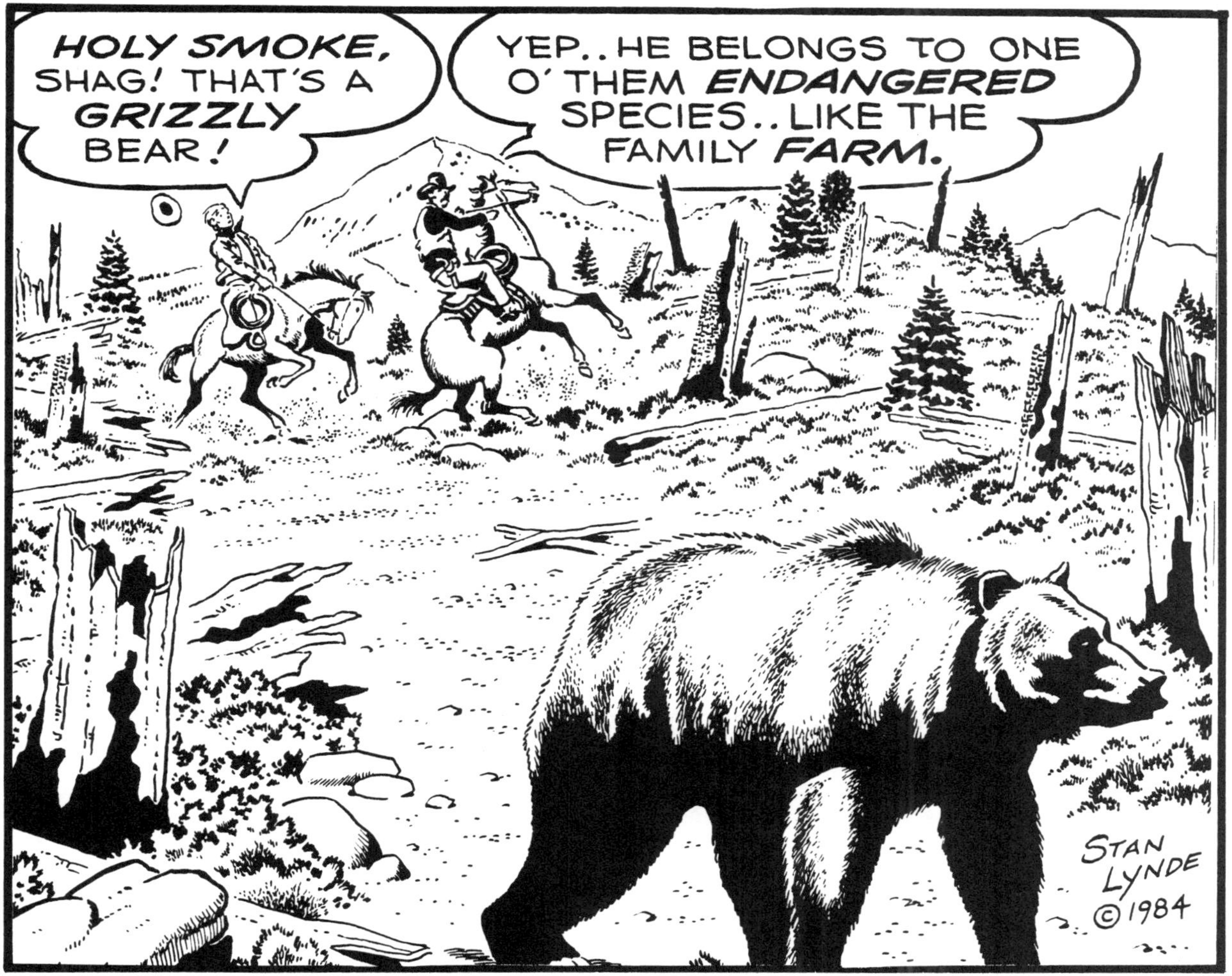
HOLY SMOKE, SHAG! THAT'S A GRIZZLY BEAR!
YEP.. HE BELONGS TO ONE O' THEM ENDANGERED SPECIES.. LIKE THE FAMILY FARM.
STAN LYNDE ©1984

What keeps the American farmer and rancher on the land in a day of increasing costs, decreasing prices, and high interest rates? What makes him continue to work and hope as his profession grows more and more uncertain?

I think it is the land itself, and the independence and freedom he perceives to be possible; he's hooked on the lifestyle.

For most, living is more important than just *making* a living, and the farmer and rancher have the satisfaction of knowing they're the best at what they do that the world has ever known.

His way of life isn't everything a man could want, maybe, but I think he'd tell you it's *most* of it.

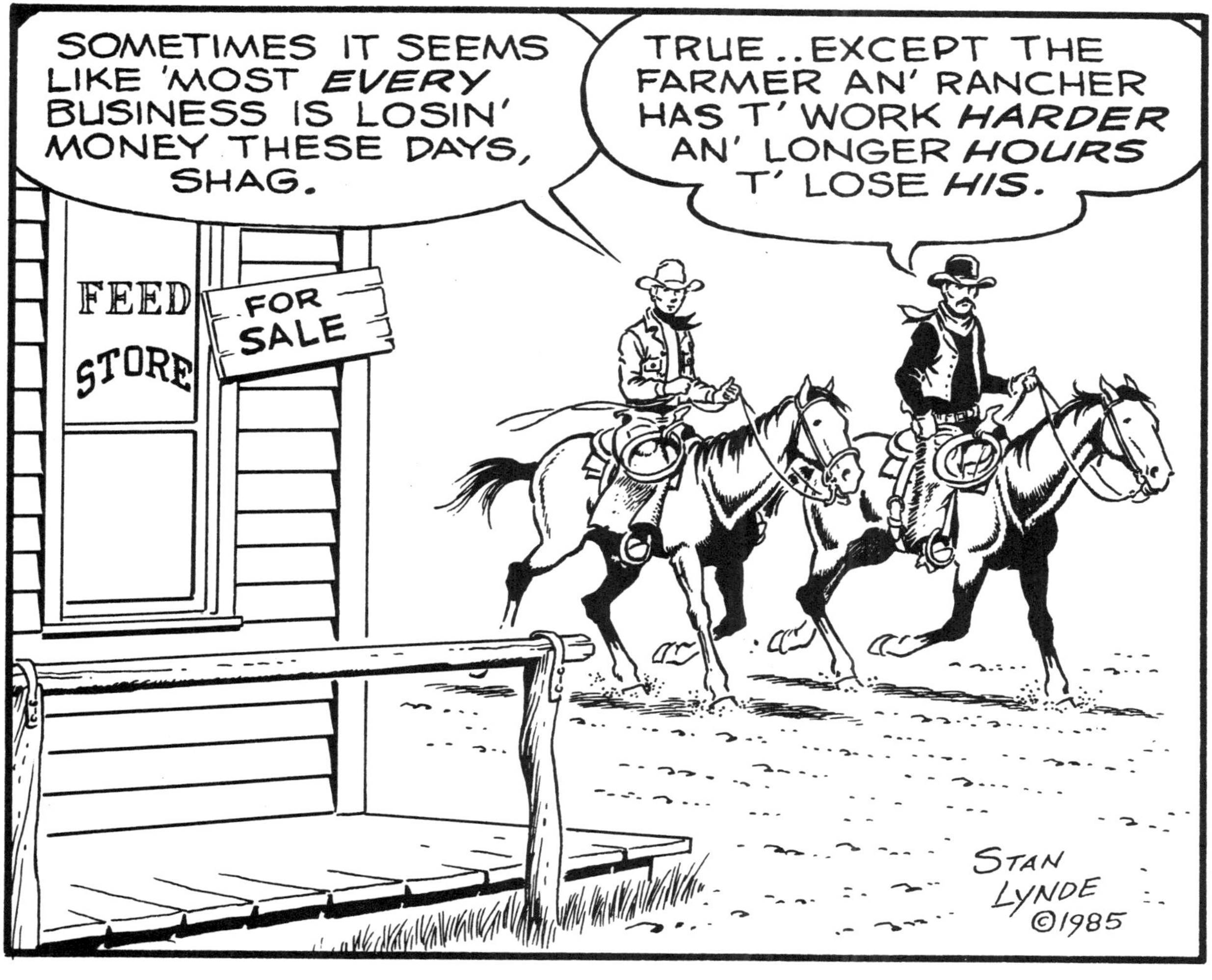
SOMETIMES IT SEEMS LIKE 'MOST EVERY BUSINESS IS LOSIN' MONEY THESE DAYS, SHAG.
TRUE..EXCEPT THE FARMER AN' RANCHER HAS T' WORK HARDER AN' LONGER HOURS T' LOSE HIS.
FEED STORE
FOR SALE
STAN LYNDE ©1985

Man's attempts to improve the land aren't always as successful as he might wish.

His efforts can succeed, as advances in soil conservation and range management have demonstrated, and progress in these areas are among the great accomplishments of farmers, ranchers, and the ASC, but I tend to be a bit leary of extravagant claims.

Like Shag, I believe the land was made perfectly just once--by its *manufacturer*.

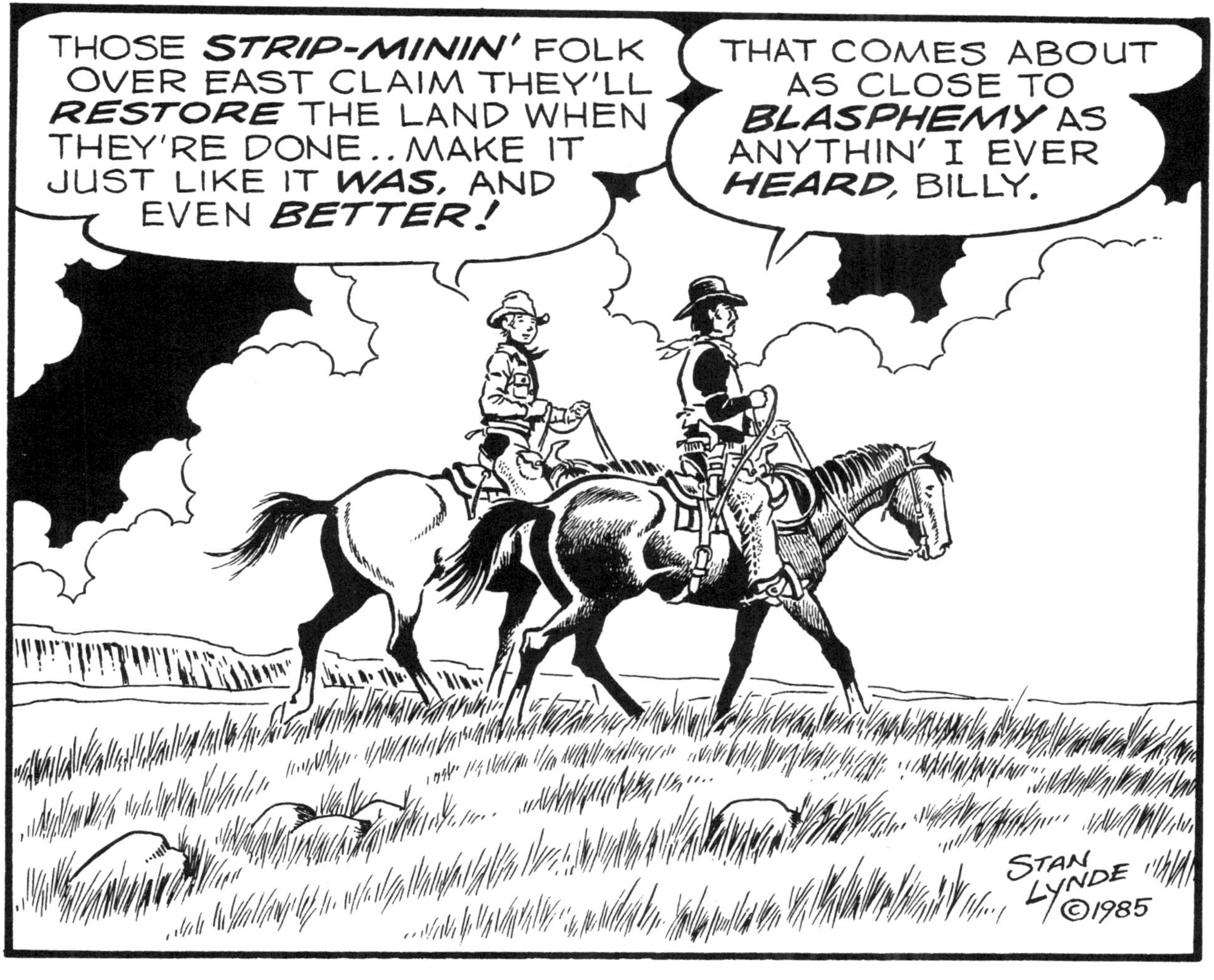
THOSE STRIP-MININ' FOLK OVER EAST CLAIM THEY'LL RESTORE THE LAND WHEN THEY'RE DONE..MAKE IT JUST LIKE IT WAS, AND EVEN BETTER!
THAT COMES ABOUT AS CLOSE TO BLASPHEMY AS ANYTHIN' I EVER HEARD, BILLY.
STAN LYNDE ©1985

I've finally stopped looking for greener pastures. My attempts to improve and control the circumstances of my life just haven't worked.

It took a long time, but I've finally come to realize that I'm *not* the Master of my Fate and the Captain of my Soul; I don't even know what my circumstances are supposed to *be!*

So I've turned all that over to the only One who can handle it and have got on with the *real* work--changing *myself.*

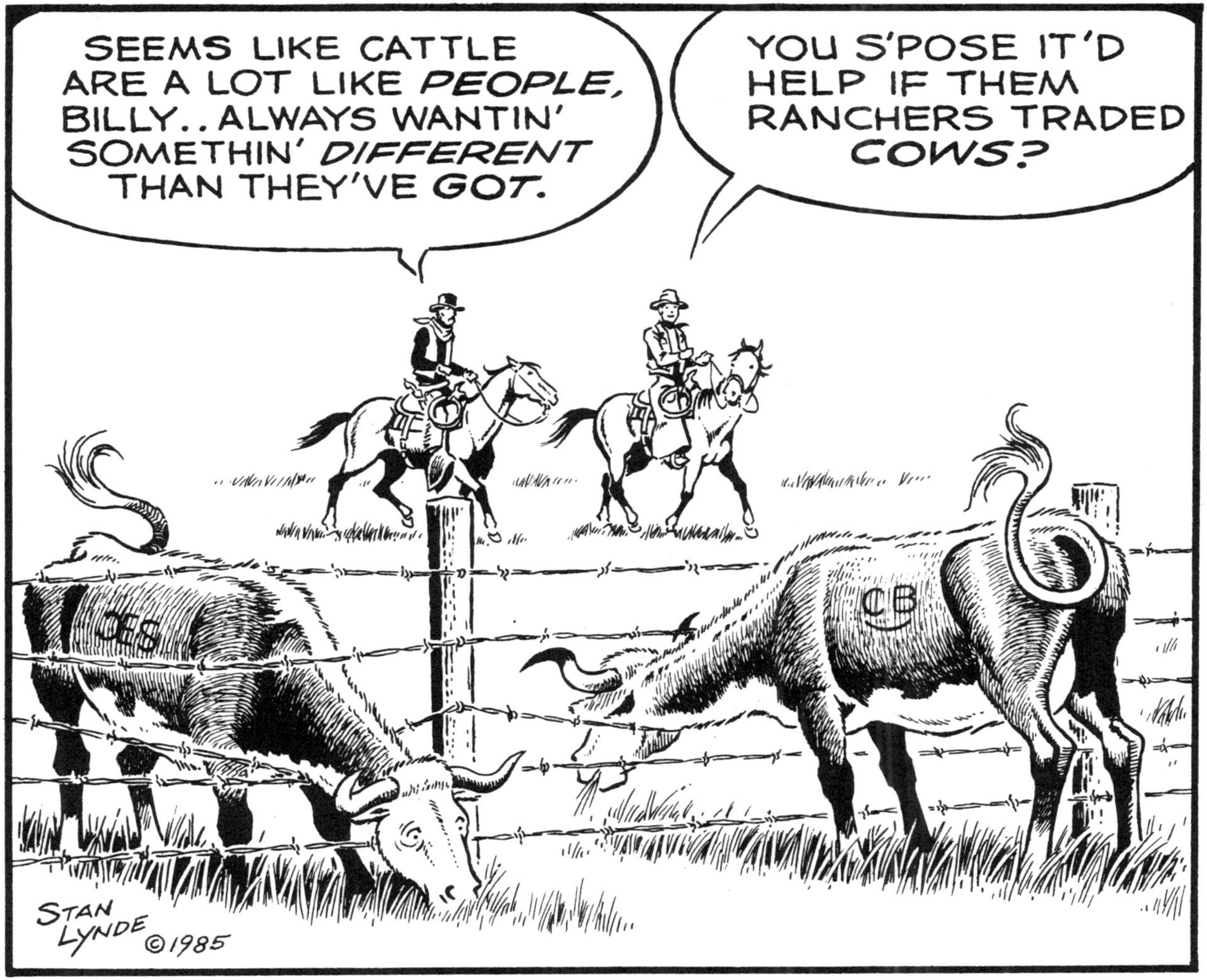
SEEMS LIKE CATTLE ARE A LOT LIKE *PEOPLE*, BILLY..ALWAYS WANTIN' SOMETHIN' *DIFFERENT* THAN THEY'VE **GOT**.
YOU S'POSE IT'D HELP IF THEM RANCHERS TRADED **COWS?**
STAN LYNDE ©1985

In every trade there are the right tools and the right way to use those tools. As long as there are cowboys the arguments will continue over whether tying hard and fast or dallying--taking wraps around the saddle horn--is best, but there is no argument over the fact that the size of the thrown loop is important.

If Billy and Shag ever *do* work elephants, they'd do well to ride big, strong horses--and use the *dally* method.

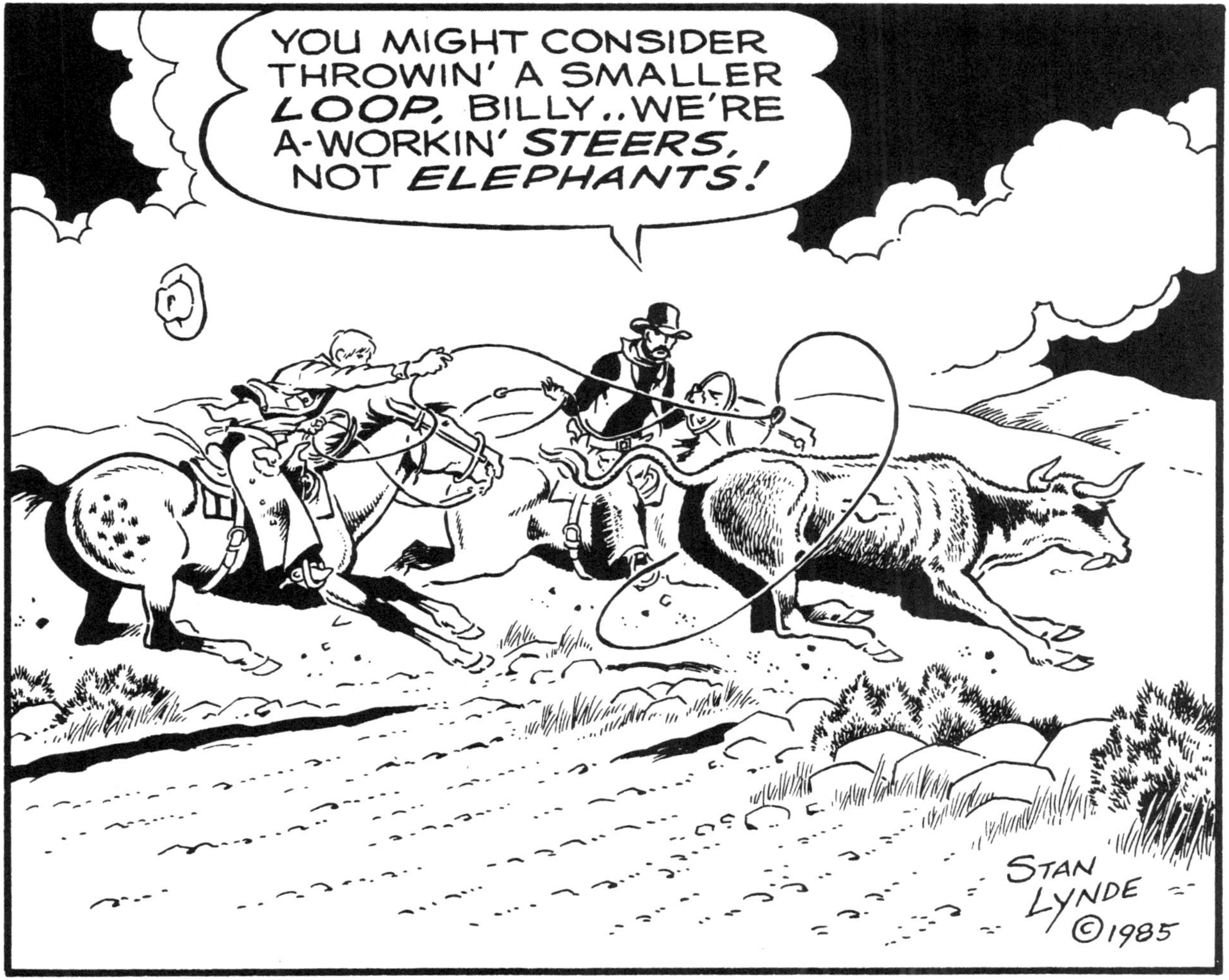
YOU MIGHT CONSIDER THROWIN' A SMALLER LOOP, BILLY..WE'RE A-WORKIN' STEERS, NOT ELEPHANTS!
STAN LYNDE ©1985

If we're going to go around asking silly questions we'd better be prepared to get some silly answers.

I don't know about you, but I still ask those dumb questions from time to time, and I'm always grateful to those exasperated people who have mercy on me and don't give me the answers I deserve.

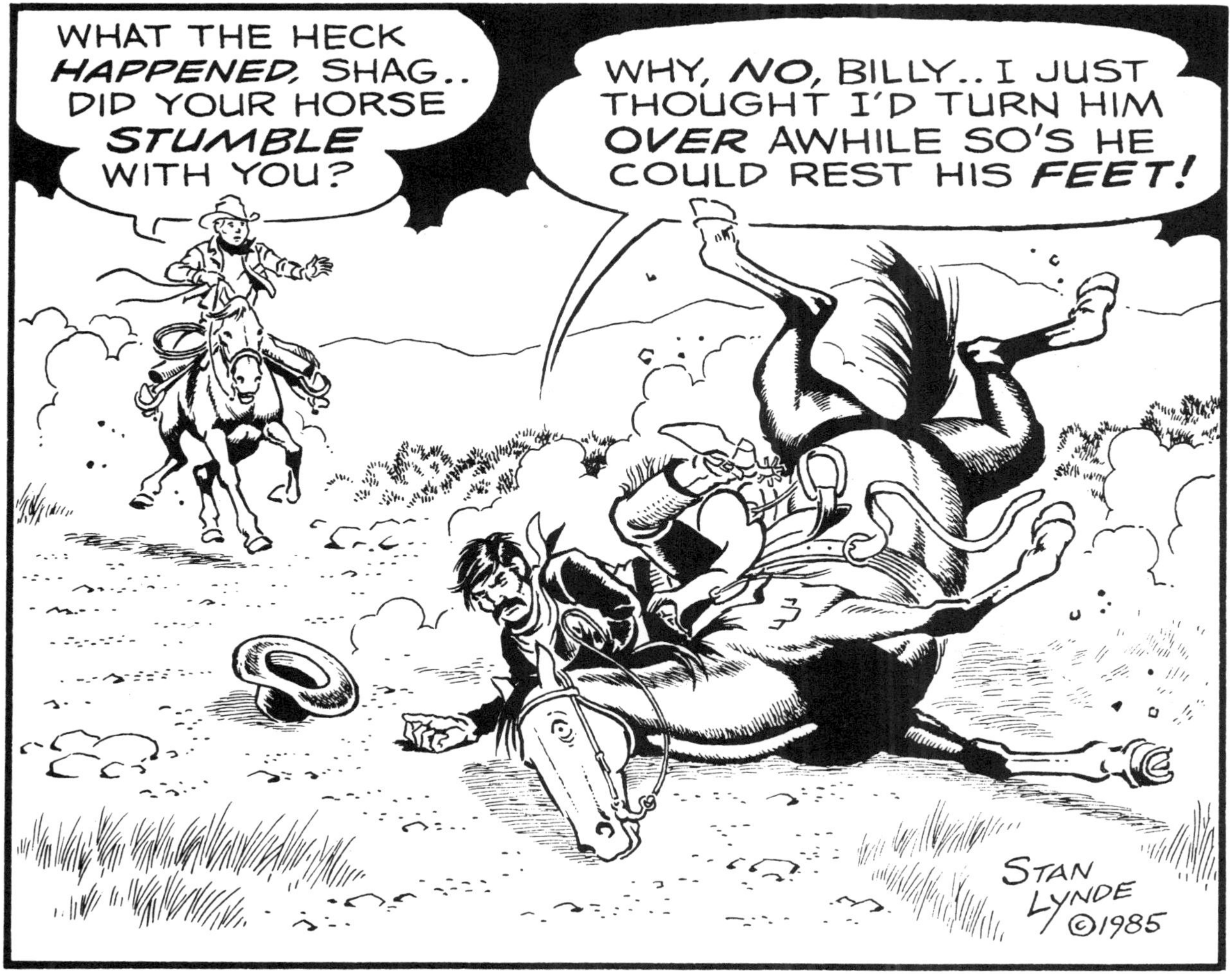
WHAT THE HECK HAPPENED, SHAG.. DID YOUR HORSE STUMBLE WITH YOU?
WHY, NO, BILLY.. I JUST THOUGHT I'D TURN HIM OVER AWHILE SO'S HE COULD REST HIS FEET!
STAN LYNDE ©1985

There's a big difference between courage and bravado.

To me, courage is doing what has to be done in a situation of risk, and minimizing that risk as much as possible. Bravado is walking barefoot through a rattlesnake convention.

Courage involves the calculated risk; bravado involves tempting fate.

I've noticed that people who are into bravado tend to get *hurt* a lot.

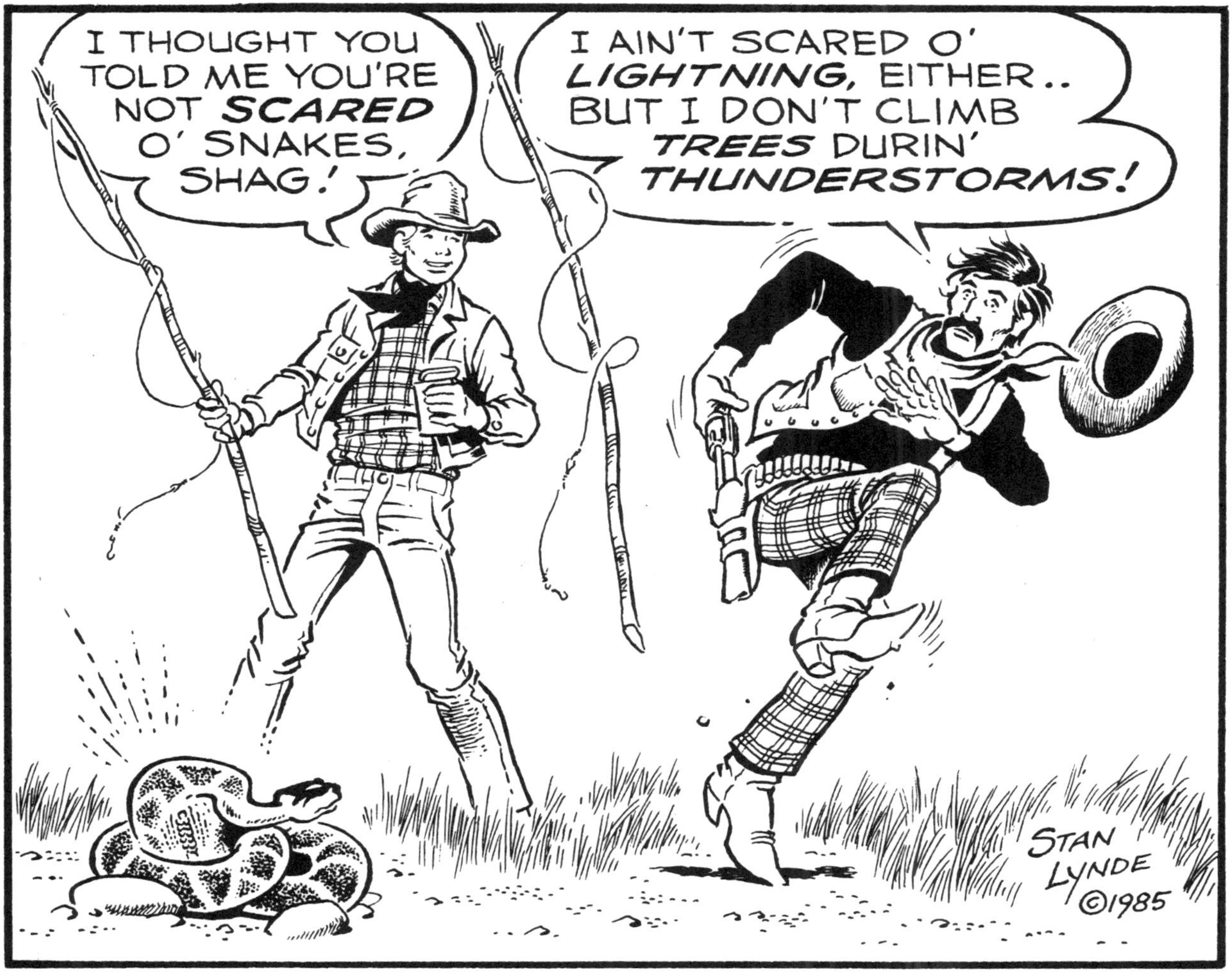
I THOUGHT YOU TOLD ME YOU'RE NOT SCARED O' SNAKES, SHAG!
I AIN'T SCARED O' LIGHTNING, EITHER.. BUT I DON'T CLIMB TREES DURIN' THUNDERSTORMS!
STAN LYNDE ©1985

I think heaven will be like all the best things we know, but infinitely greater--a whole new dimension of joy and peace we can't even imagine because we don't yet have the equipment to do so.

I think we are given *hints* in this life, little previews of that greater existence--a child's smile, shared laughter, an understanding friend, a spectacular sunrise.

For me, mountains and the feelings they give me are some of God's greatest hints.

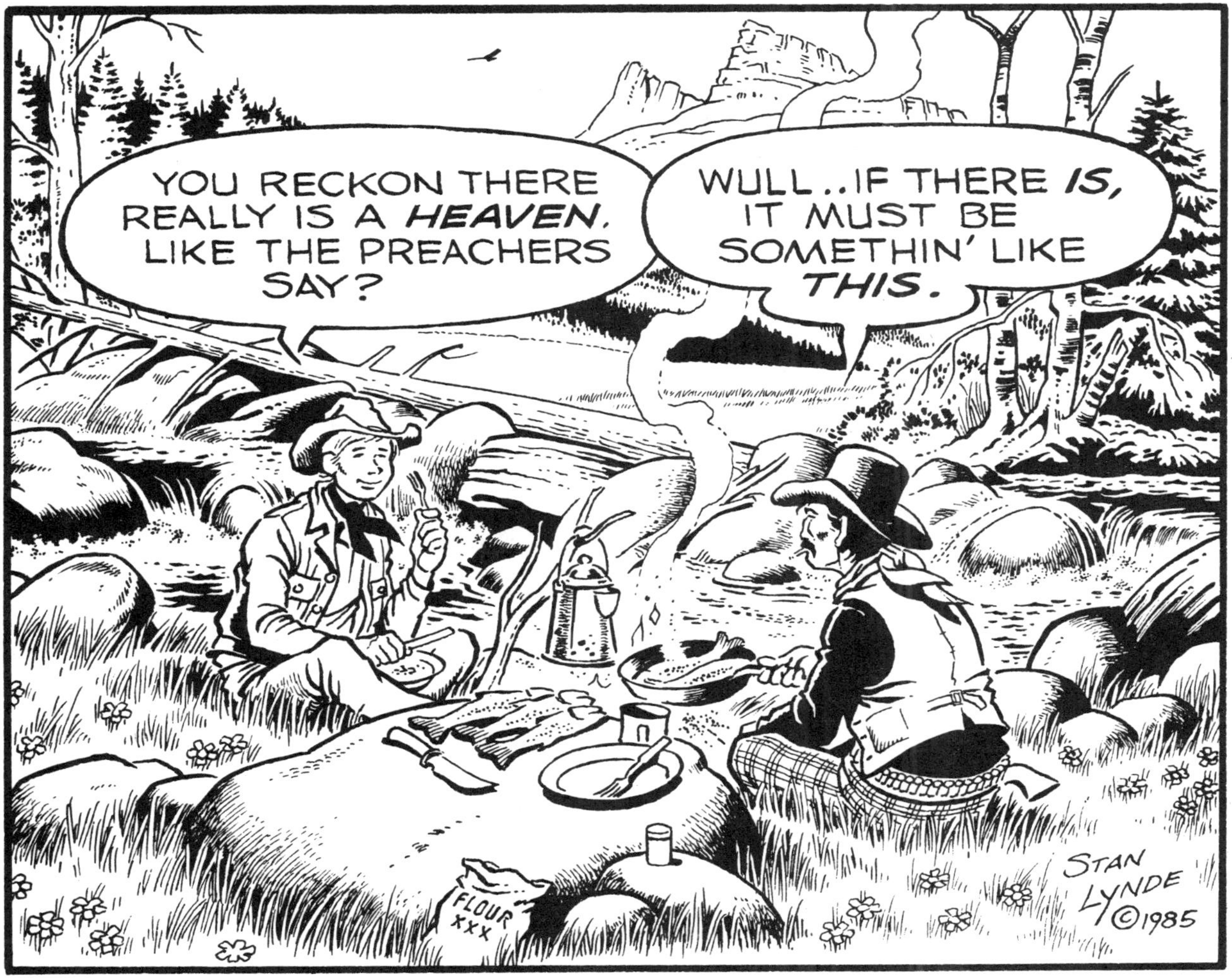
YOU RECKON THERE REALLY IS A *HEAVEN*, LIKE THE PREACHERS SAY?
WULL..IF THERE *IS*, IT MUST BE SOMETHIN' LIKE *THIS*.
FLOUR XXX
STAN LYNDE ©1985

The old-time cowboy was above all a horseman; the rider and his mount were a single unit designed for a single purpose--working cattle. It was part of a cowboy's pride that he was a rider, and he often felt uneasy and less than complete out of the saddle.

He wasn't lazy; he just felt disdain and sympathy for us lesser mortals who make our livings on our feet or at a desk.

Or at a drawing board.

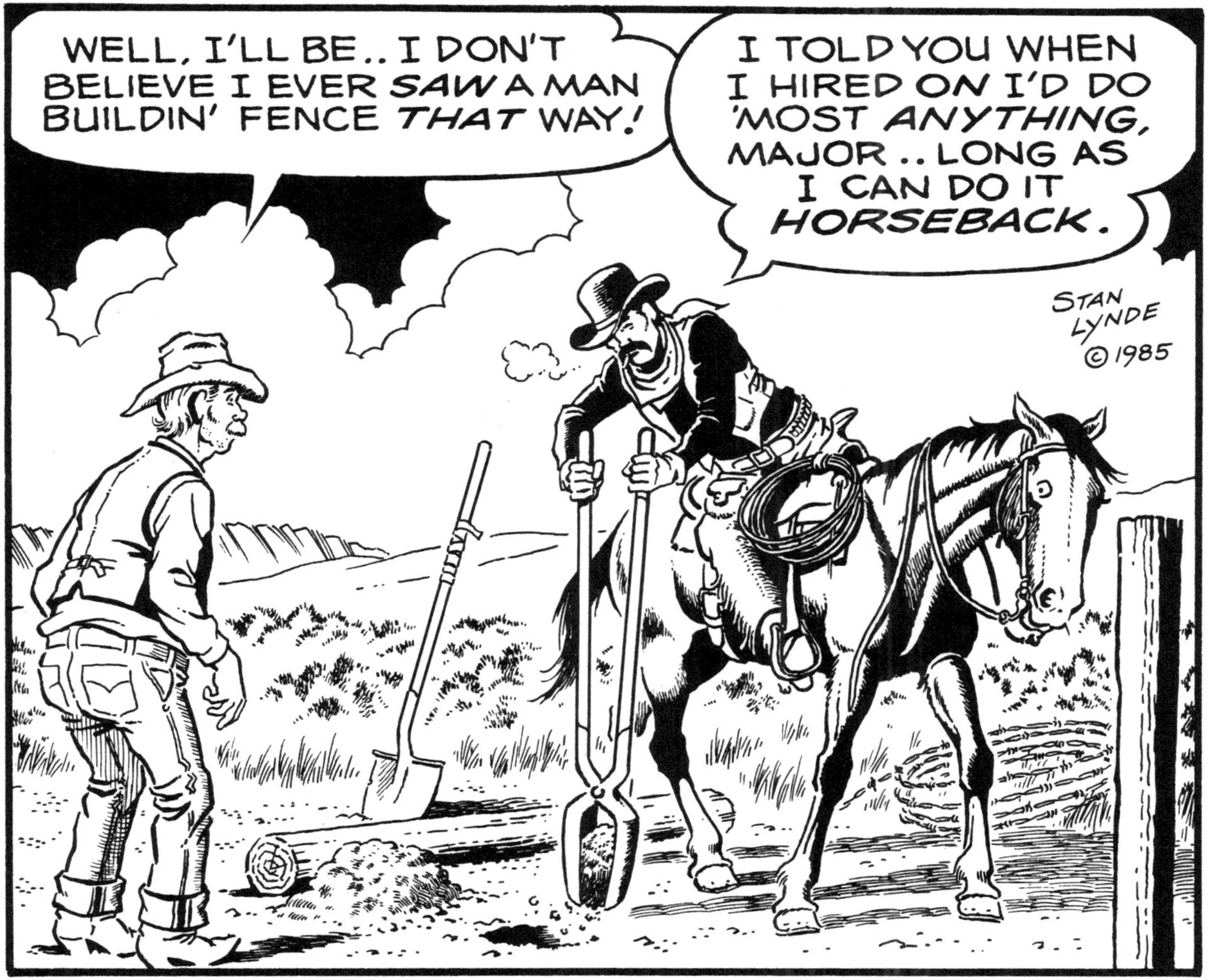
WELL, I'LL BE.. I DON'T BELIEVE I EVER SAW A MAN BUILDIN' FENCE THAT WAY!
I TOLD YOU WHEN I HIRED ON I'D DO 'MOST ANYTHING, MAJOR .. LONG AS I CAN DO IT HORSEBACK.
STAN LYNDE © 1985

I don't agree with the person who complained that youth is wasted on the young, but I have both marveled at and envied their seemingly unlimited energy.

I'd like to believe that we're only as old as we feel, and that feeling youthful and energetic are within our control.

I'd *like* to believe that.

The older I get, the *more* I'd like to believe that.

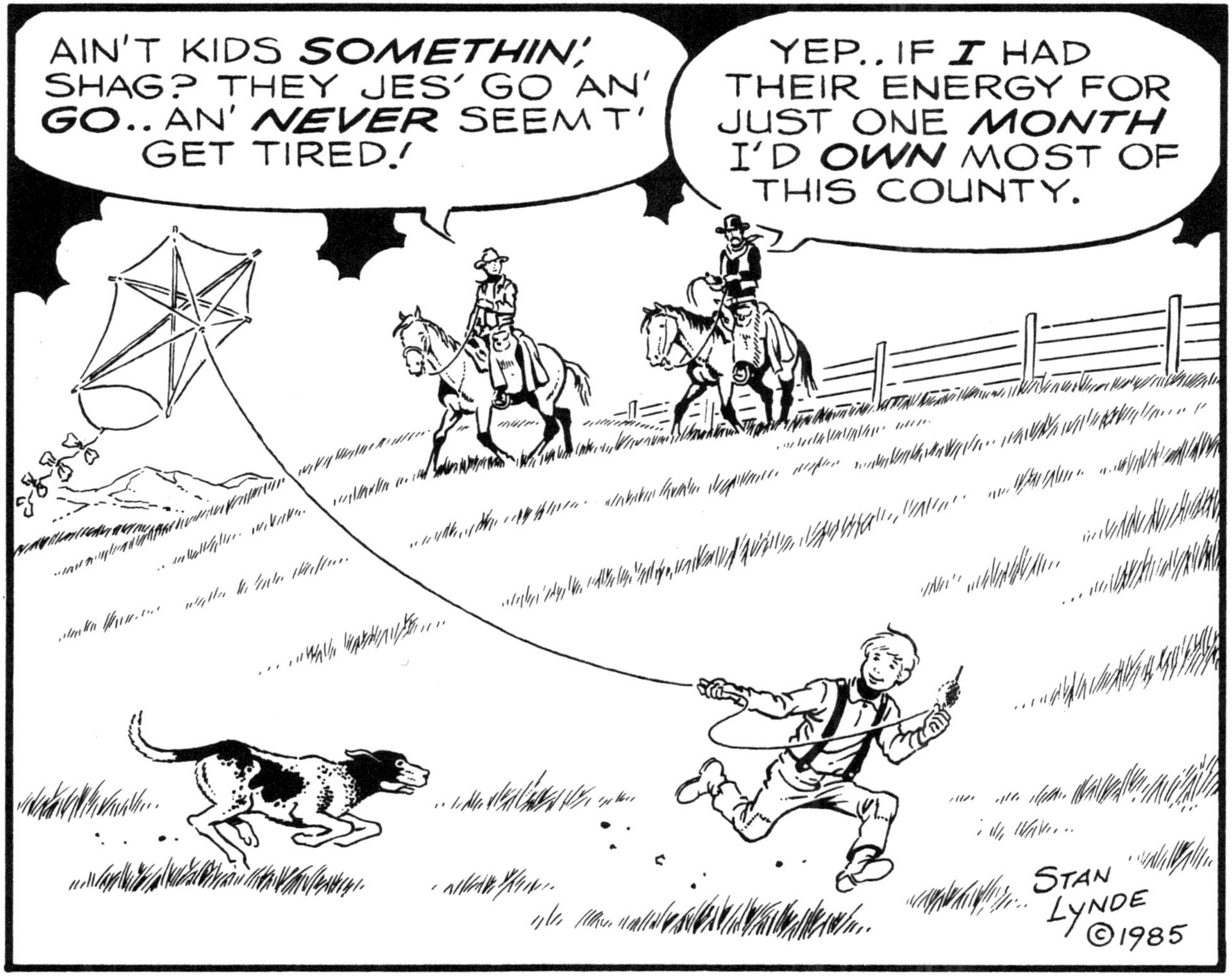
AIN'T KIDS SOMETHIN', SHAG? THEY JES' GO AN' GO.. AN' NEVER SEEM T' GET TIRED!
YEP.. IF I HAD THEIR ENERGY FOR JUST ONE MONTH I'D OWN MOST OF THIS COUNTY.
STAN LYNDE ©1985

I never fail to be amazed at the things I think I know--things I'm positively, unshakeably *sure* of--that just aren't so.

It's always a surprise when I learn I've held a false idea so firmly for so long, and I get a little uneasy as I wonder what *else* I'm sure of that isn't true.

Times like those sure do tend to keep me humble, though, and that's good--I can use all the humility I can *get*.

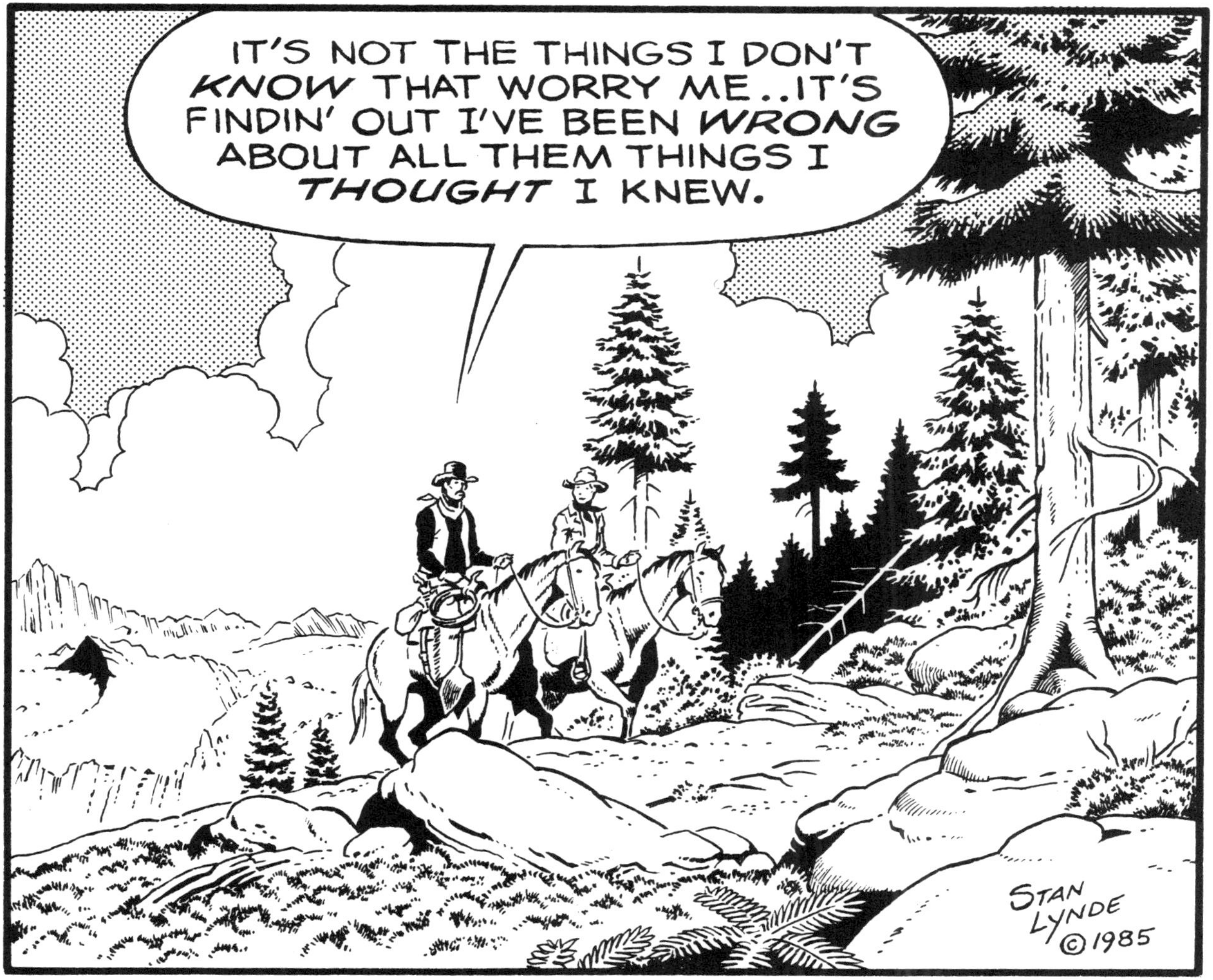
IT'S NOT THE THINGS I DON'T *KNOW* THAT WORRY ME..IT'S FINDIN' OUT I'VE BEEN *WRONG* ABOUT ALL THEM THINGS I *THOUGHT* I KNEW.
STAN LYNDE ©1985

Freedom is a quality that can easily be taken for granted, and I think it's worth an occasional reminder that we enjoy more of it as Americans than anyone else on earth.

Our freedom isn't free; it has cost us the lives of the best of our young men from Lexington to Da Nang, and it's preserved only by our being willing to pay the price in the future.

We preserve it, too, by keeping ourselves informed and aware, and by voting in our local, state, and national elections. Our right to vote was *also* bought with a price.

Every profession and lifestyle has its drawbacks, but as Americans we're free to choose our own.

For us, freedom is not an *option;* it's a *necessity.*

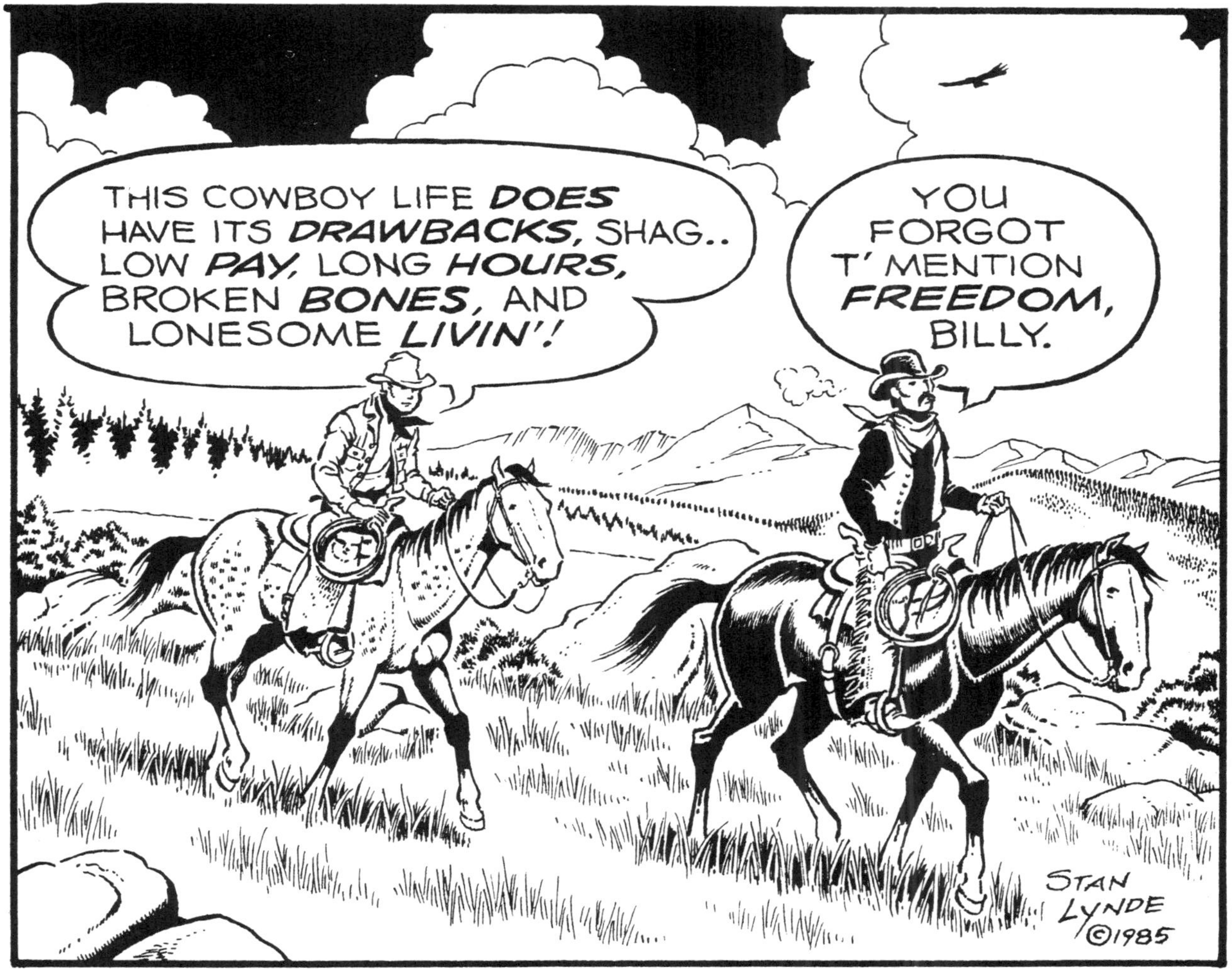
THIS COWBOY LIFE DOES HAVE ITS DRAWBACKS, SHAG.. LOW PAY, LONG HOURS, BROKEN BONES, AND LONESOME LIVIN'!
YOU FORGOT T' MENTION FREEDOM, BILLY.
STAN LYNDE ©1985

During nearly every political campaign some office-seeker vows to balance the budget, and I think we can be excused by now if some of us have stopped *believing* that particular promise.

If a balanced budget is a myth, then our defecit is a nightmare, and I sometimes wish politicians would quit talking about *either* if they're not going to *do* something about them.

When you and I go into debt, we tighten our belts, get a second job, work harder, and worry a lot.

When the government goes in debt, it prints more *money*.

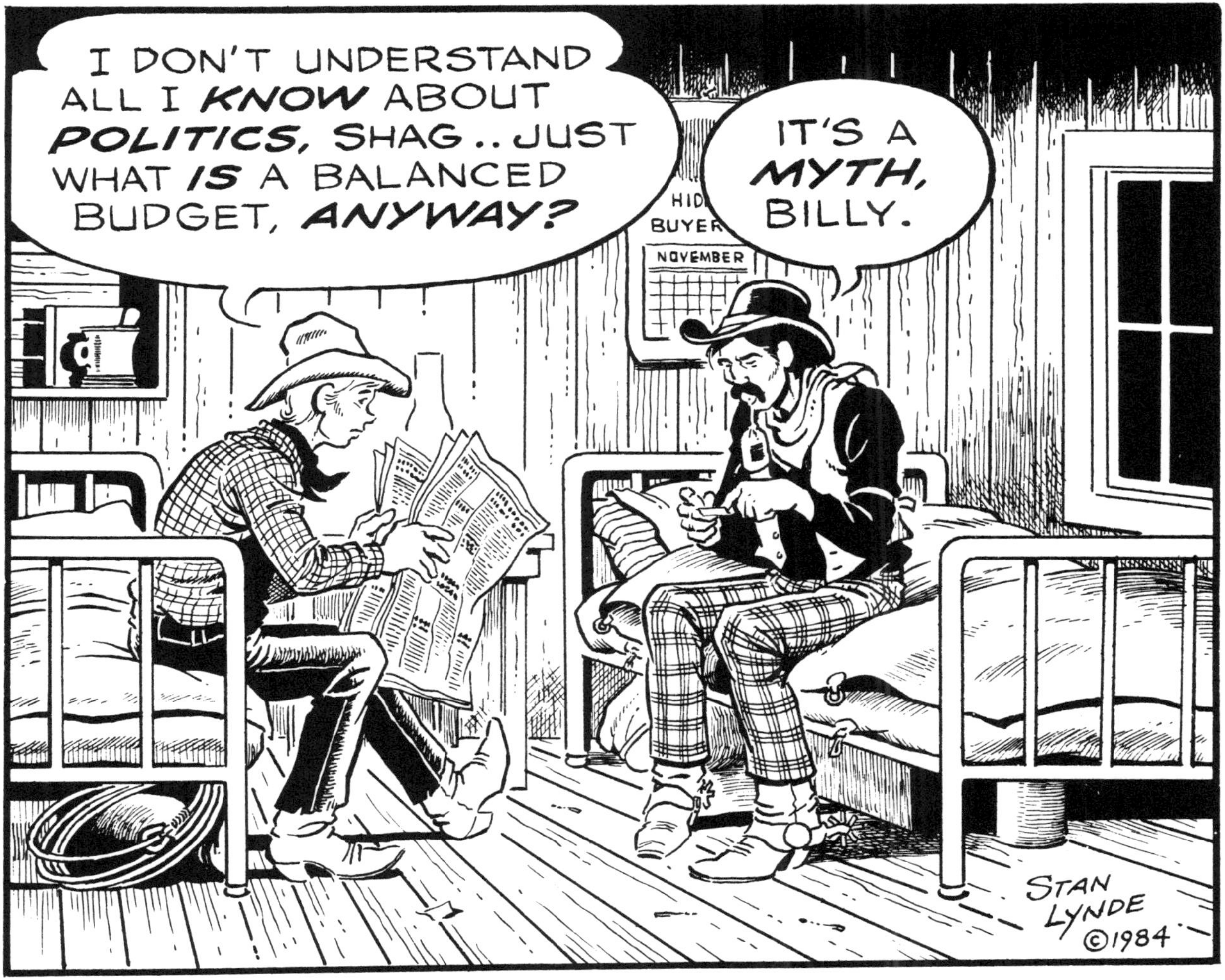
I DON'T UNDERSTAND ALL I KNOW ABOUT POLITICS, SHAG.. JUST WHAT IS A BALANCED BUDGET, ANYWAY?
IT'S A MYTH, BILLY.
HID
BUYER
NOVEMBER
STAN LYNDE ©1984

Inflation is when workers demand more money so they can pay higher prices for stuff made by manufacturers so the manufacturers can raise their prices to pay their workers more so they can pay higher prices ...

There *must* be a better way.

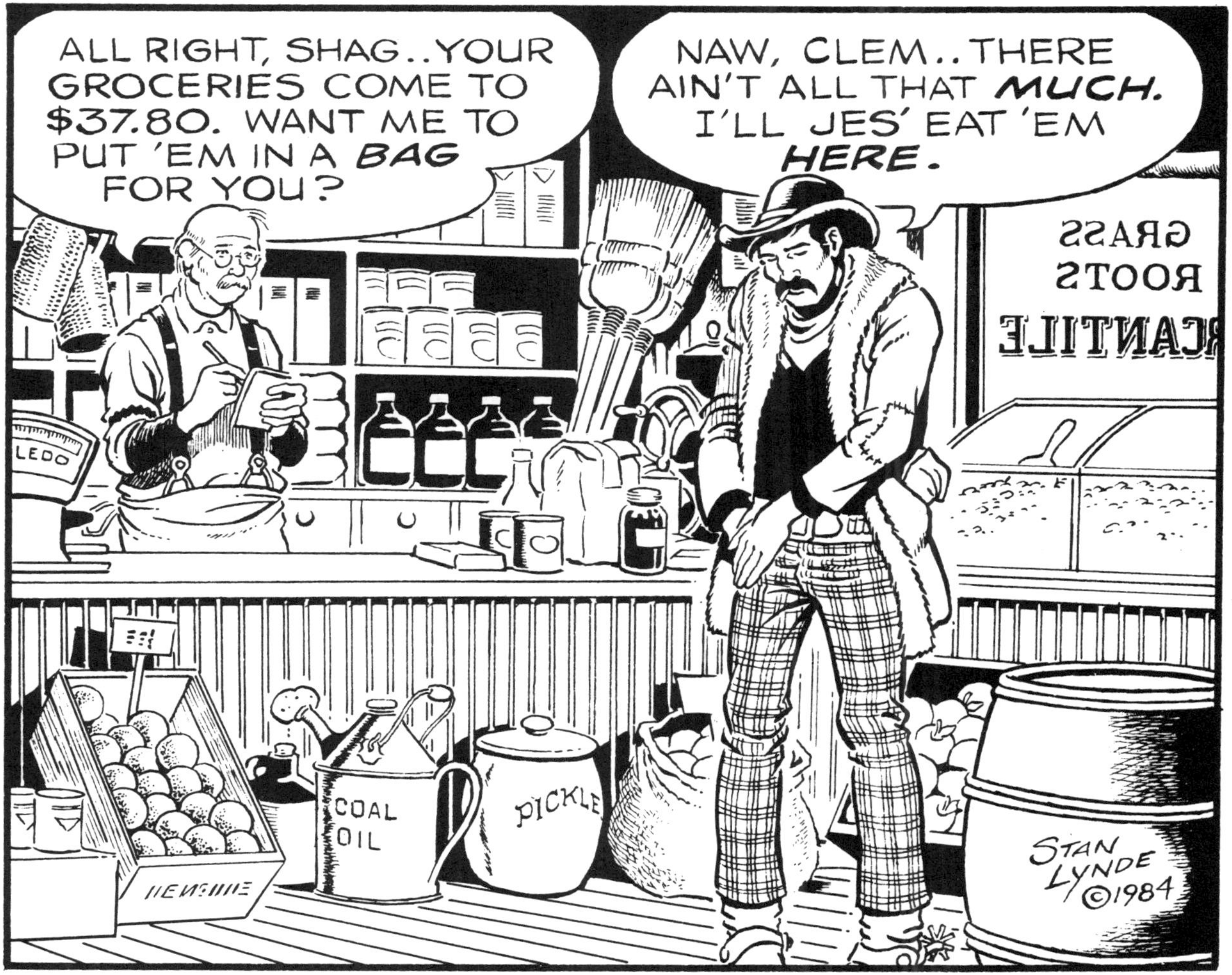
ALL RIGHT, SHAG..YOUR GROCERIES COME TO $37.80. WANT ME TO PUT 'EM IN A BAG FOR YOU?
NAW, CLEM..THERE AIN'T ALL THAT MUCH. I'LL JES' EAT 'EM HERE.
GRASS ROOTS
COAL OIL
PICKLE
STAN LYNDE ©1984

In the Riddle and Gregg musical *Cowboy* there's a line from a song which goes:

"It isn't a face-off with death that'll kill you; it's a slip of your memory for livin' that plants you down deep."

It has been said that eternal vigilance is the price of liberty, and I'd say that applies to other things as well. A man has the right to get careless around a green, nervous bronc if he wants to, but he should understand that there's a price-tag for every right.

Sometimes, *pain* is nature's way of telling us to be more *careful.*

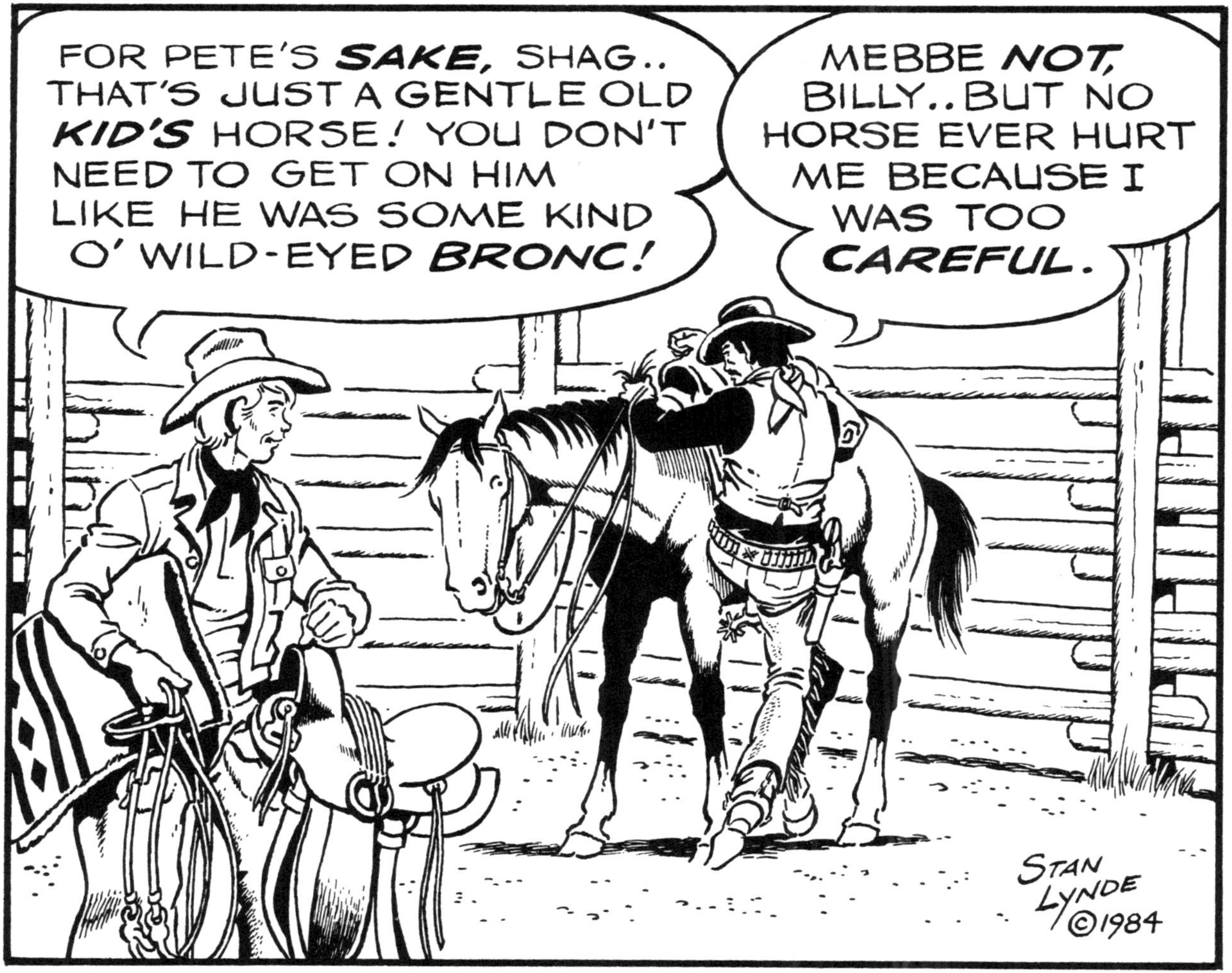
FOR PETE'S SAKE, SHAG.. THAT'S JUST A GENTLE OLD KID'S HORSE! YOU DON'T NEED TO GET ON HIM LIKE HE WAS SOME KIND O' WILD-EYED BRONC!
MEBBE NOT, BILLY..BUT NO HORSE EVER HURT ME BECAUSE I WAS TOO CAREFUL.
STAN LYNDE ©1984

I'm certainly in favor of protecting the rights of the accused; I think we all should be, because none of us can be sure the time won't come when we'll *be* the accused.

But I am in favor of a certain balance. It doesn't make sense to me that the rights of a criminal should be the subject of greater concern than the rights of his *victim,* nor that the people we pay to protect us all should be handicapped in the performance of that difficult job.

When my dad raised sheep on the reservation, he hunted coyotes with a pack of greyhounds.

I can't remember that he ever *hobbled* or *muzzled* them.

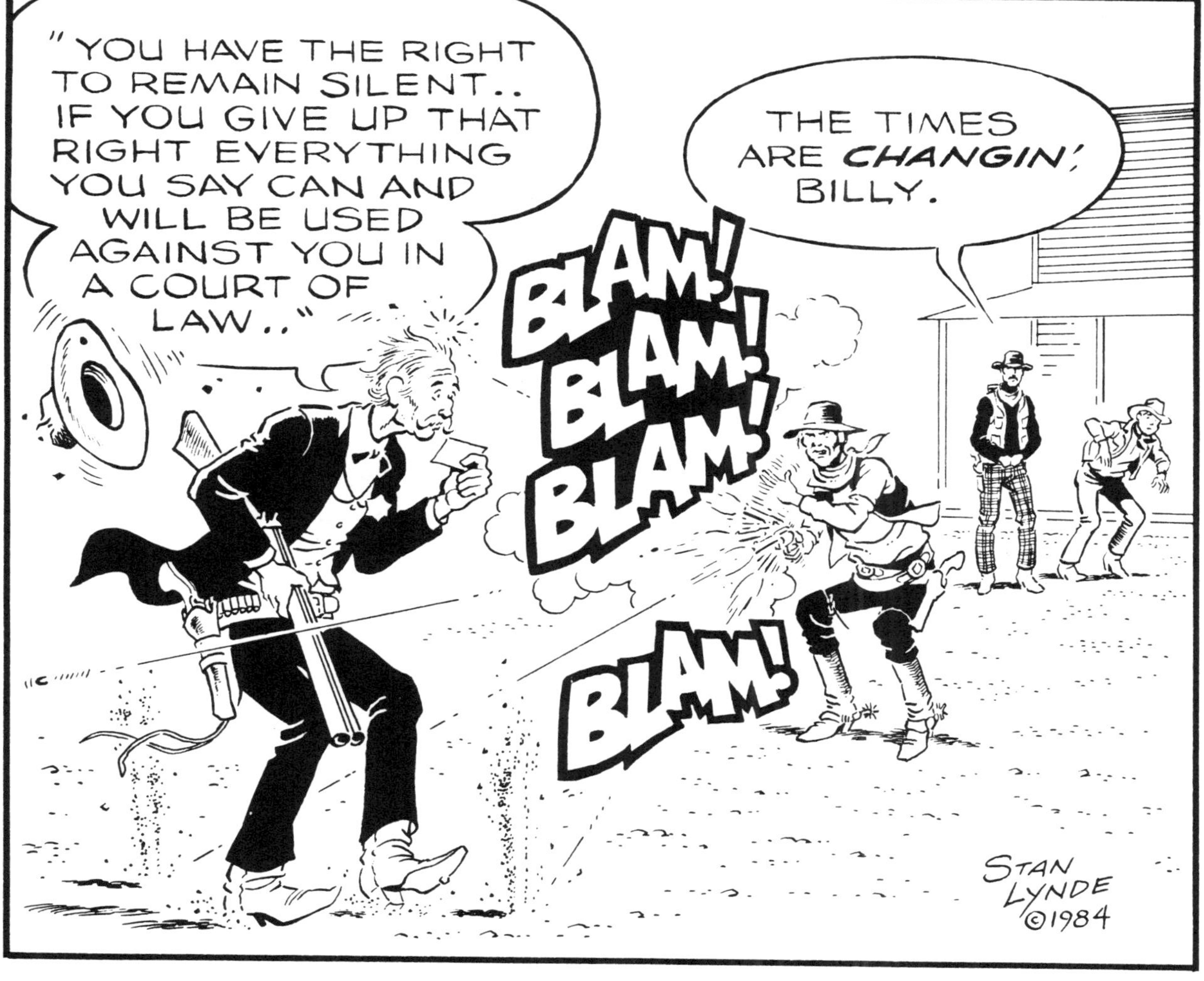
"YOU HAVE THE RIGHT TO REMAIN SILENT.. IF YOU GIVE UP THAT RIGHT EVERYTHING YOU SAY CAN AND WILL BE USED AGAINST YOU IN A COURT OF LAW.."
THE TIMES ARE *CHANGIN'*, BILLY.
BLAM! BLAM! BLAM!
BLAM!
STAN LYNDE ©1984

At long last, some attention is now being paid to victim's rights, and I find that an encouraging trend.

Certainly, confinement behind the cold, grey walls of an overcrowded prison is a grim, hard fate, but then so is the suffering, mental anguish, and continuing trauma which is often the lot of the victim.

Society requires laws, and it needs to enforce those laws with justice and compassion, but I think it must be at *least* as compassionate and concerned for the criminal's victim.

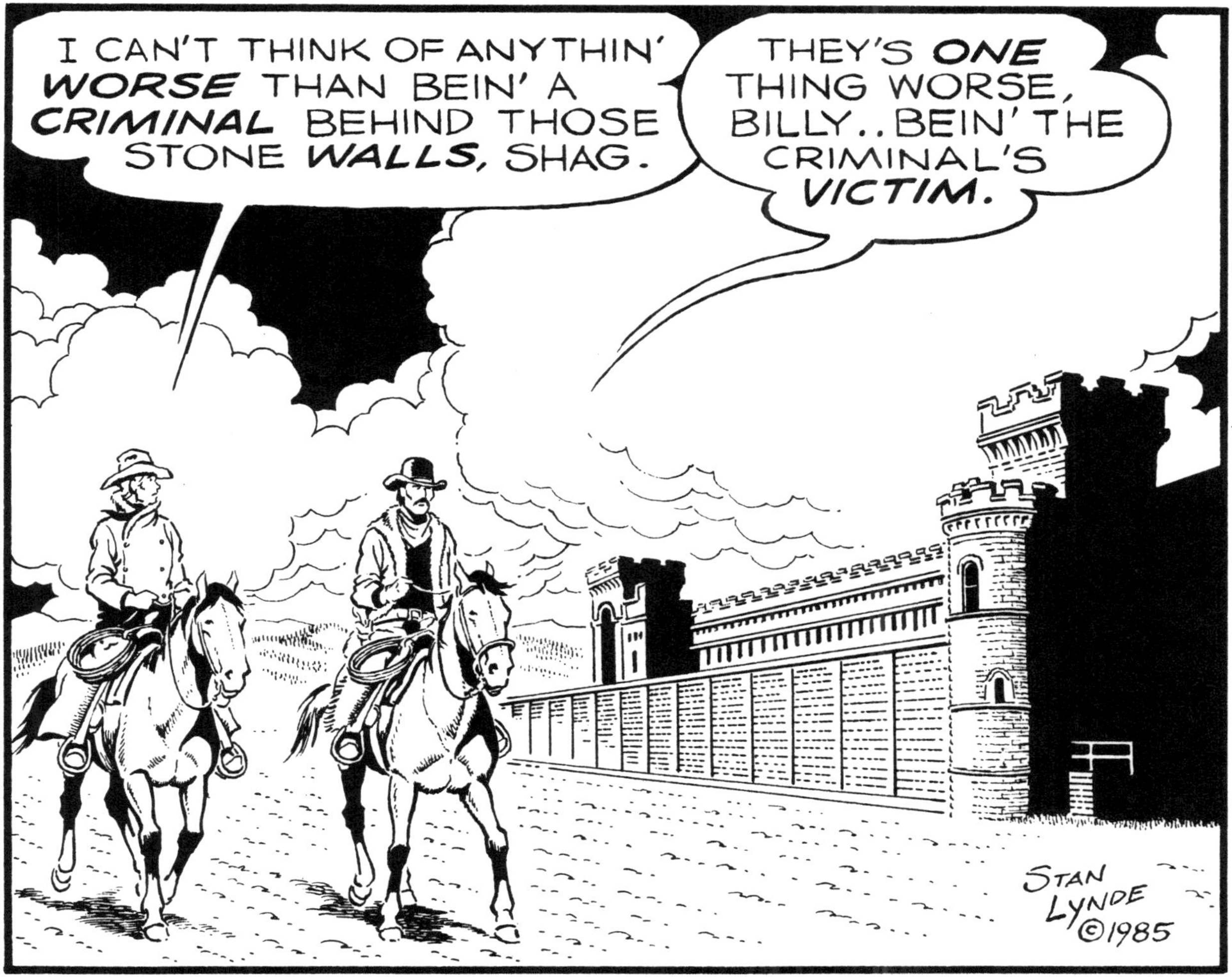
I CAN'T THINK OF ANYTHIN' *WORSE* THAN BEIN' A *CRIMINAL* BEHIND THOSE STONE *WALLS*, SHAG.
THEY'S *ONE* THING WORSE, BILLY.. BEIN' THE CRIMINAL'S *VICTIM*.
STAN LYNDE ©1985

No Hollywood producer ever enjoyed his Beverly Hills pool as much as my friend Dale and I did a muddy reservoir on the plains above Beauvais Creek. After a hot day tying fleece and stomping wool at shearing time, that sagebrush and cactus bordered pond felt like a blue lagoon in the south seas at sunset.

Like Billy and Shag, we had spectators--livestock, meadowlarks, magpies, and prairie dogs who no doubt wondered what two teen-age kids were doing in their drinking water.

To the best of my knowledge, our evening swims caused no harm to any of the reservoir's rightful users, and they did *us* a lot of *good*.

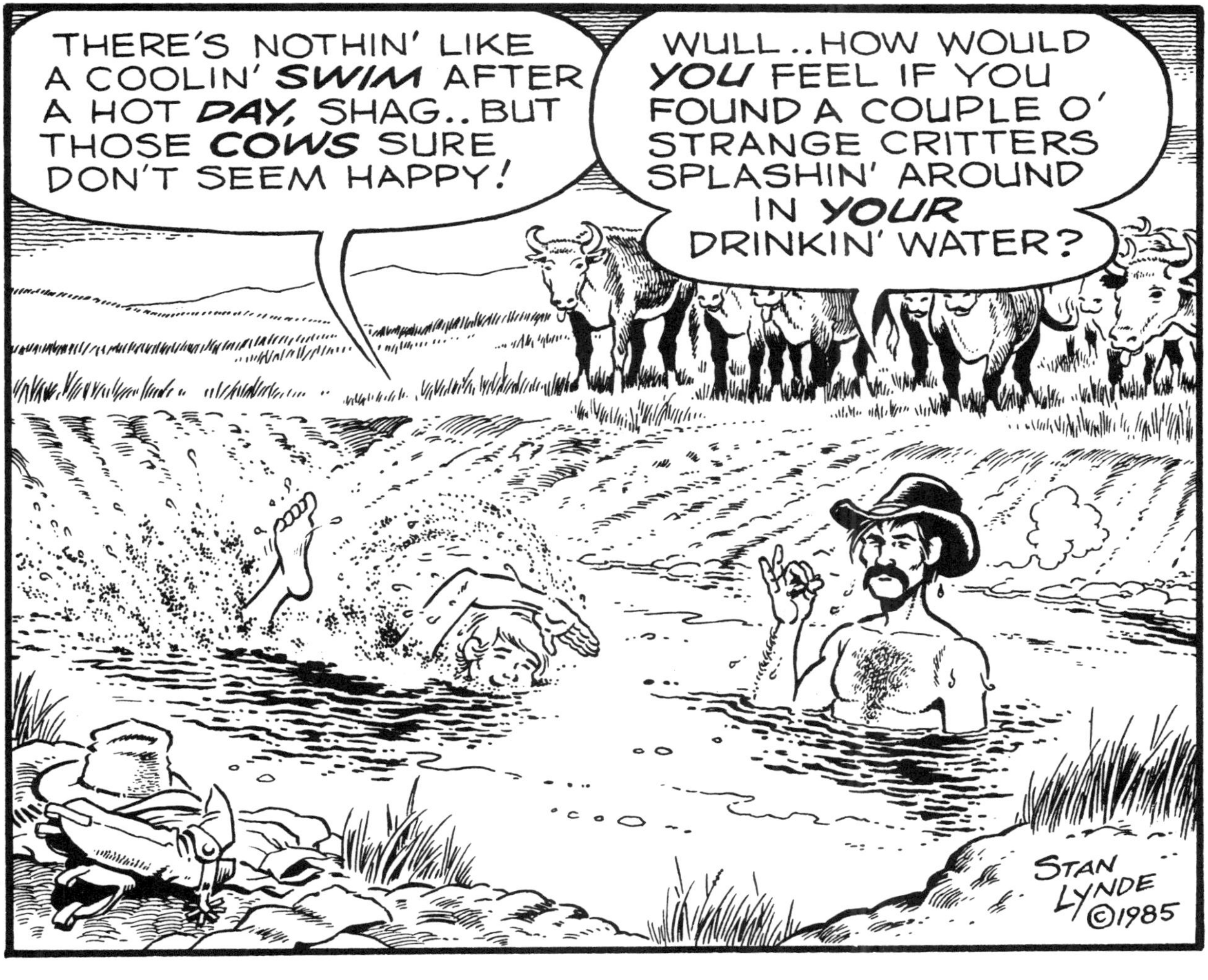
THERE'S NOTHIN' LIKE A COOLIN' SWIM AFTER A HOT DAY, SHAG.. BUT THOSE COWS SURE DON'T SEEM HAPPY!
WULL.. HOW WOULD YOU FEEL IF YOU FOUND A COUPLE O' STRANGE CRITTERS SPLASHIN' AROUND IN YOUR DRINKIN' WATER?
STAN LYNDE ©1985

Like other depression-era kids, I've seen grasshopper invasions which literally wiped out an entire year of my parents' hard work. They came in great clouds, eating everything--crops, leaves, even leather and wood. They were everywhere--in vehicles, in barns and sheds, in our house and in our hair--and they left destruction and devastation in their wake.

Modern insecticides have helped to control the problem in recent years, but the hoppers still come. And while they aren't *really* big enough to hunt with a .30-.30, they make up in appetite what they may lack in size.

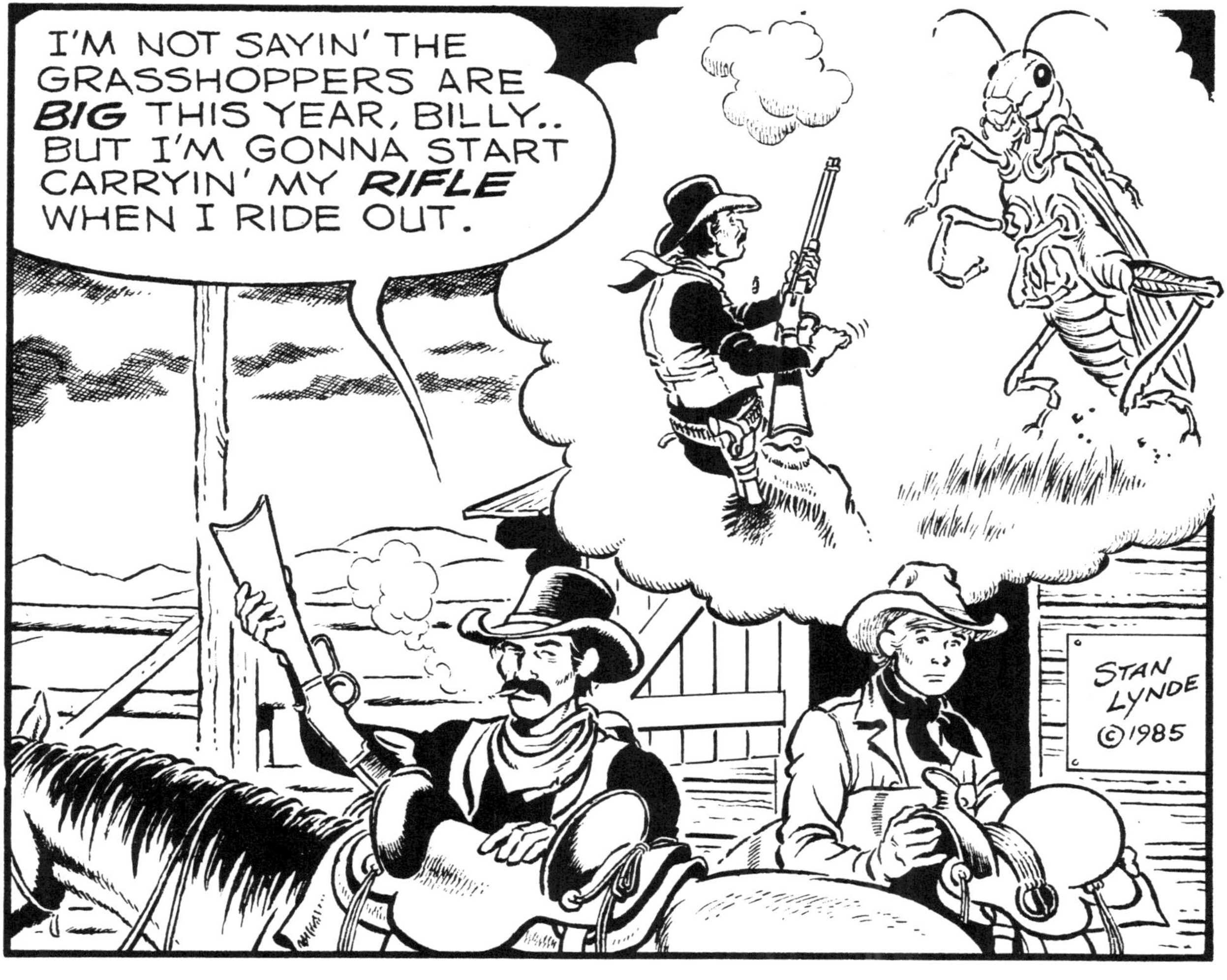
I'M NOT SAYIN' THE GRASSHOPPERS ARE **BIG** THIS YEAR, BILLY.. ..BUT I'M GONNA START CARRYIN' MY **RIFLE** WHEN I RIDE OUT.
STAN LYNDE ©1985

Watching a long-time rancher negotiate with an experienced cattle or sheep buyer used to be something like watching Wild Bill Hickok face down John Wesley Hardin, or playing a good game of poker. Not only were the negotiations deadly serious from a business standpoint, they were also recreation and a test of skill for both eavesdroppers and participants.

The stakes were high, and Dame Fortune dealt the cards. But win, lose, or draw the game would be played out again next year, with a new deck and the same players.

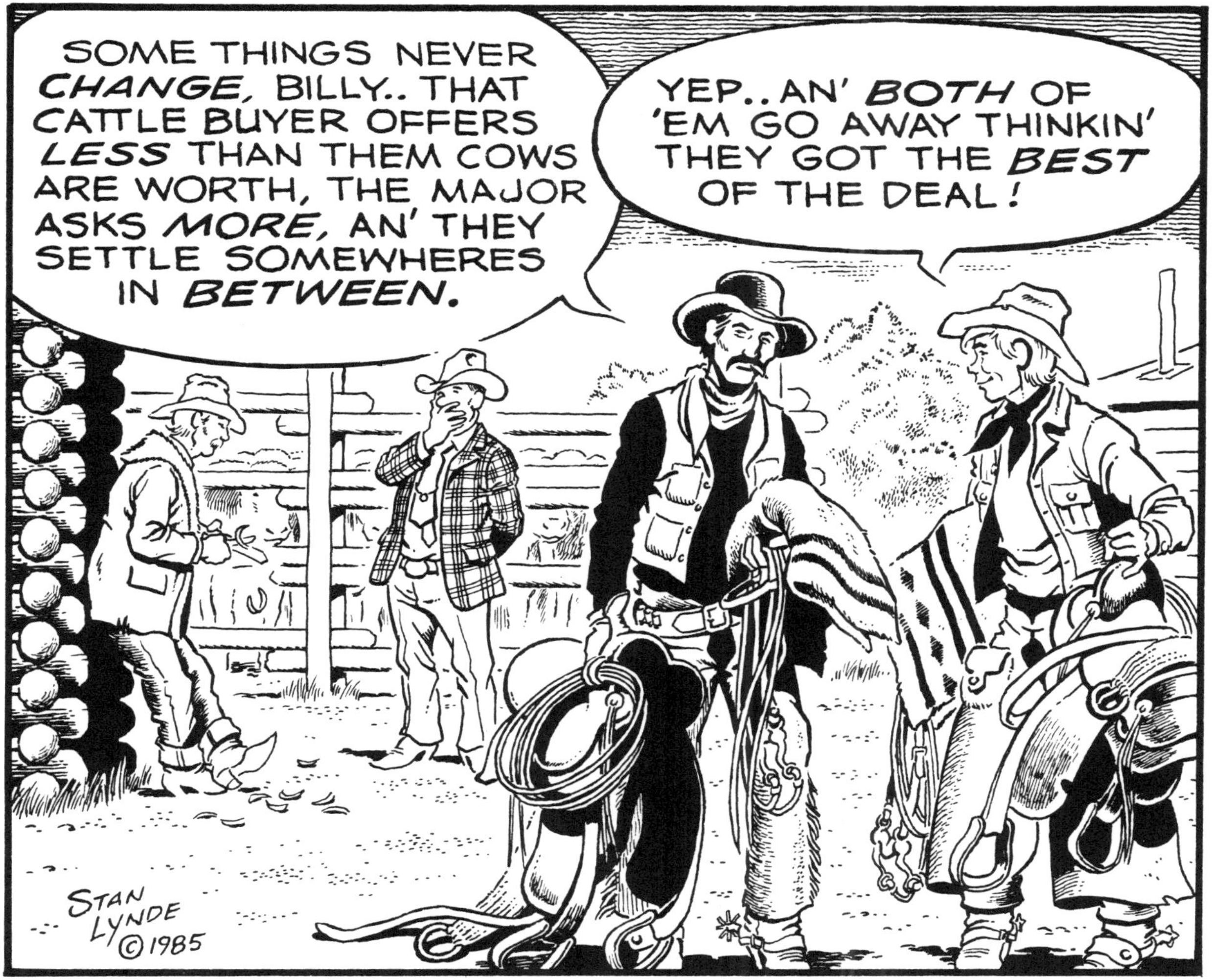
SOME THINGS NEVER CHANGE, BILLY.. THAT CATTLE BUYER OFFERS LESS THAN THEM COWS ARE WORTH, THE MAJOR ASKS MORE, AN' THEY SETTLE SOMEWHERES IN BETWEEN.
YEP.. AN' BOTH OF 'EM GO AWAY THINKIN' THEY GOT THE BEST OF THE DEAL!
STAN LYNDE ©1985

Shag has a point; Billy has at least paid all his bills, with something left over.

The government, on the other hand, keeps on finding new areas that require spending, and it keeps on increasing its indebtedness.

Come to think of it, farmers and ranchers have a lot in common with the government.

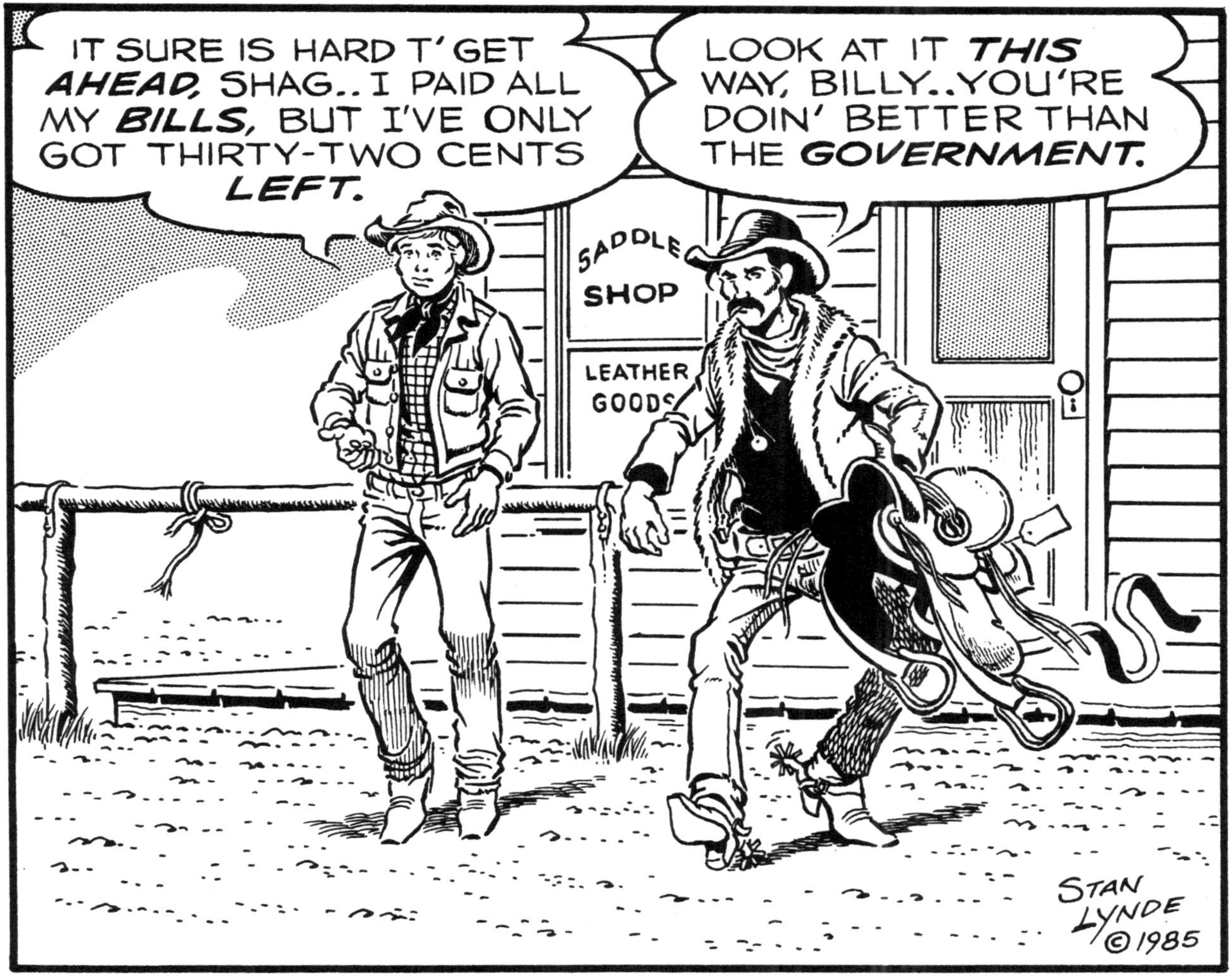
IT SURE IS HARD T' GET AHEAD, SHAG.. I PAID ALL MY BILLS, BUT I'VE ONLY GOT THIRTY-TWO CENTS LEFT.
LOOK AT IT THIS WAY, BILLY..YOU'RE DOIN' BETTER THAN THE GOVERNMENT.
SADDLE SHOP
LEATHER GOODS
STAN LYNDE © 1985

A famous writer once pointed out that Americans tend to deny death; we somehow seem to believe that if we do everything just right we'll live forever, all prior evidence to the contrary.

Comparing us to the Spanish, he went on to say that they, as a people, are more realistic. "They know that death is simply a part of life," he wrote, "and by far the *longer* part."

That we will all definitely face death should cause us to look more carefully at how we live now, and to pay more attention to that "longer part." Depending on our genes and our habits, the day will come for all of us; only the date, place, and final cause are unknown.

"Don't take life too serious," goes the cowboy wisdom, "we ain't gonna get out of it alive *anyhow.*"

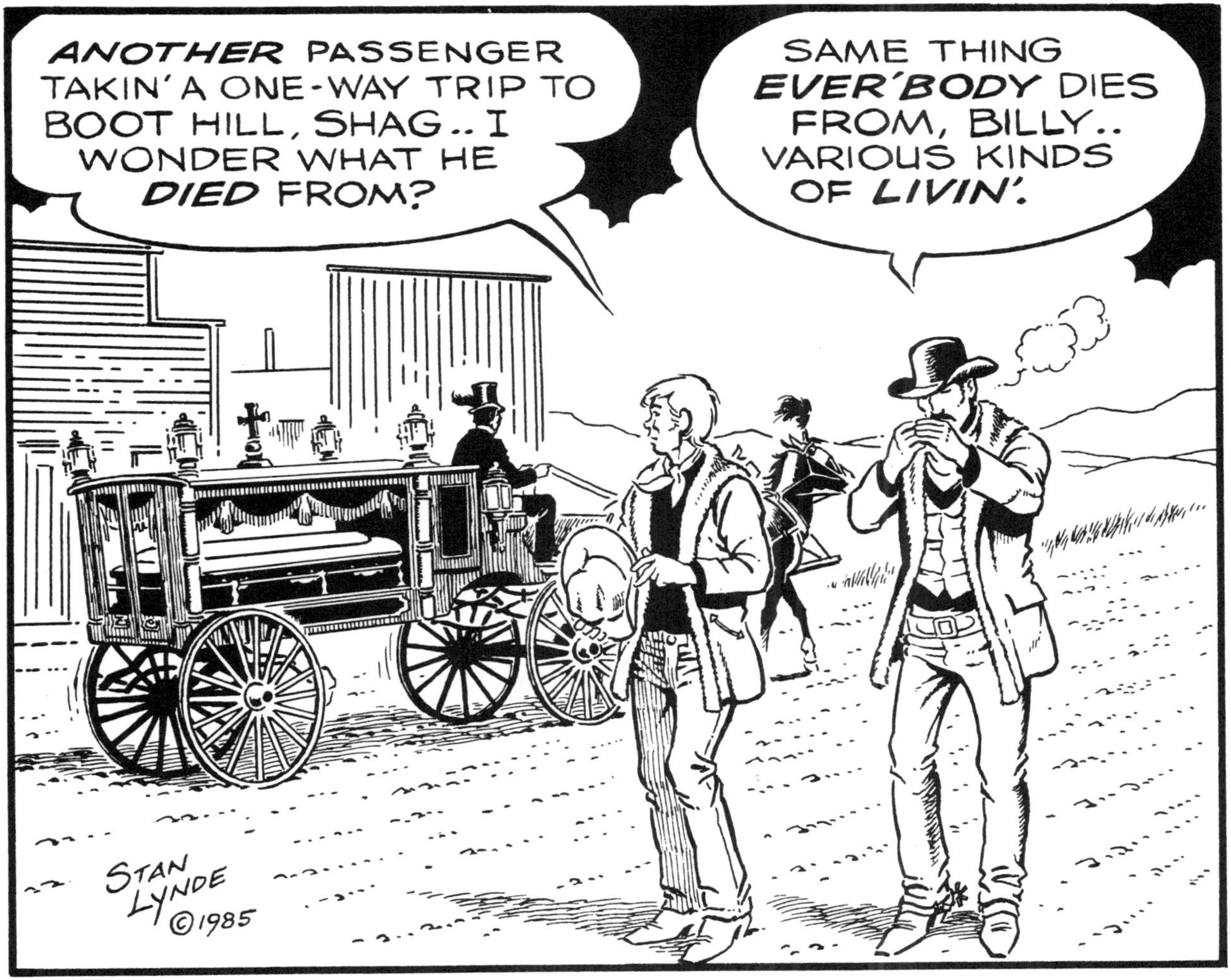
ANOTHER PASSENGER TAKIN' A ONE-WAY TRIP TO BOOT HILL, SHAG.. I WONDER WHAT HE DIED FROM?
SAME THING EVER'BODY DIES FROM, BILLY.. VARIOUS KINDS OF LIVIN'.
STAN LYNDE ©1985

Many a recovering alcoholic has discovered that his life only really *began* with sobriety. Some have even declared that they're grateful they *are* alcoholics, because through their addiction they arrived at the crisis point which brought them to a new way of life in which serenity, personal growth, spiritual enlightenment, and a real joy of living fill each day.

It has been said that we develop good judgment through experience, and that we gain experience through *bad* judgment. Life is filled with experiences and challenges, with times of joy and times of pain, and each of these is an opportunity for us to learn, grow, and to become the people we were meant to be.

At the very least, we delay that growth when we go through our lives anesthetized.

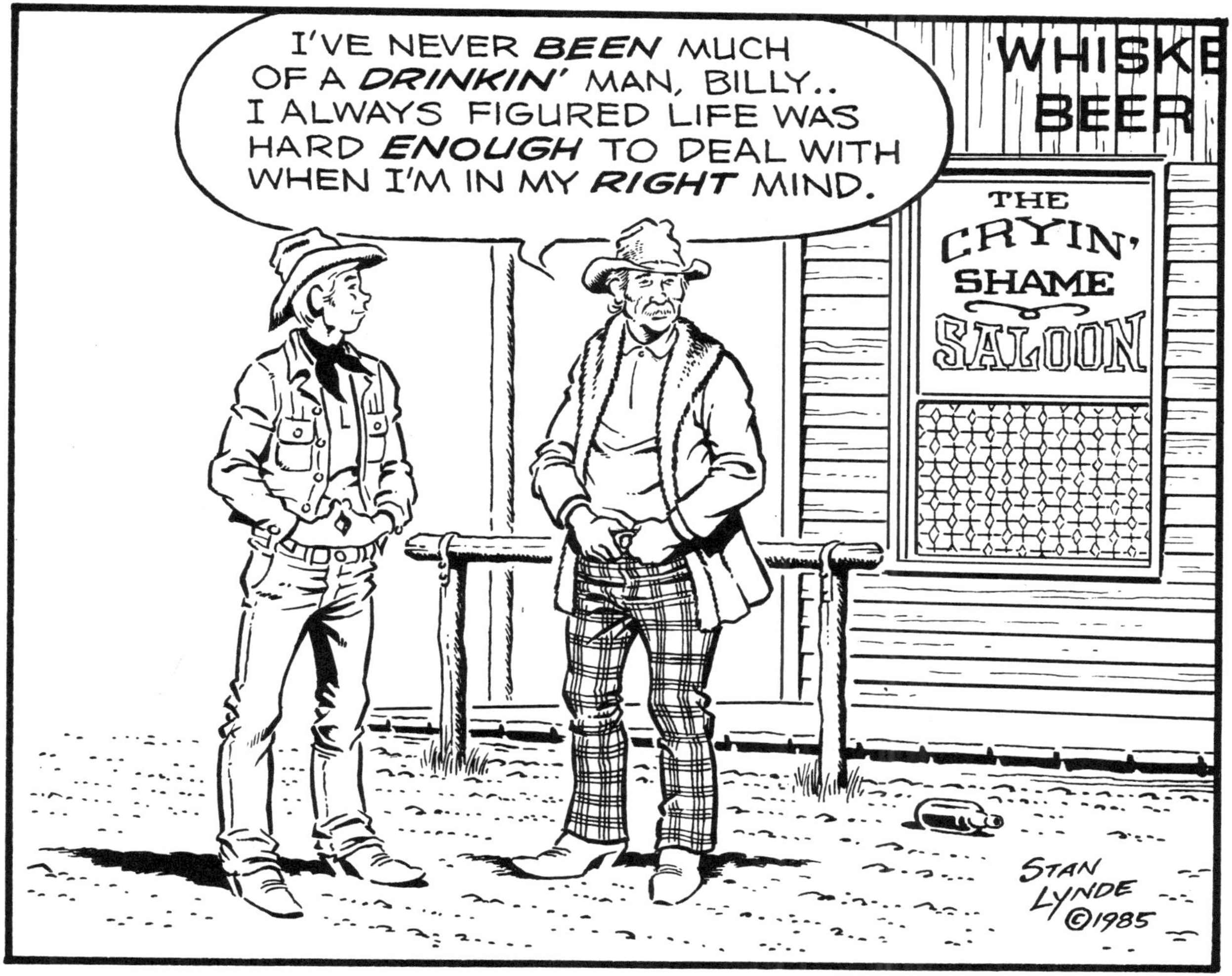
I'VE NEVER BEEN MUCH OF A DRINKIN' MAN, BILLY.. I ALWAYS FIGURED LIFE WAS HARD ENOUGH TO DEAL WITH WHEN I'M IN MY RIGHT MIND.
WHISKE
BEER
THE CRYIN' SHAME SALOON
STAN LYNDE ©1985

"Nothing is sure in life except death and taxes," goes the old saying, but I think I'd add crime to that short list, as well.

Crime does seem to be growing, in spite of the dedication, technological advances, and improved training methods of modern law enforcement. Our court calendars are jammed, as are our overcrowded, inadequate prisons, and the taxpayer pays more each year to apprehend, prosecute, and confine the criminal.

Some see the problem as a conflict between law enforcement and liberal courts; others view it as a result of societal and environmental failure.

I don't know the answer, either, but I am convinced it won't be found in any changes in the laws or legal system. If answers there be, I believe they'll be found only in the changed hearts and minds of people.

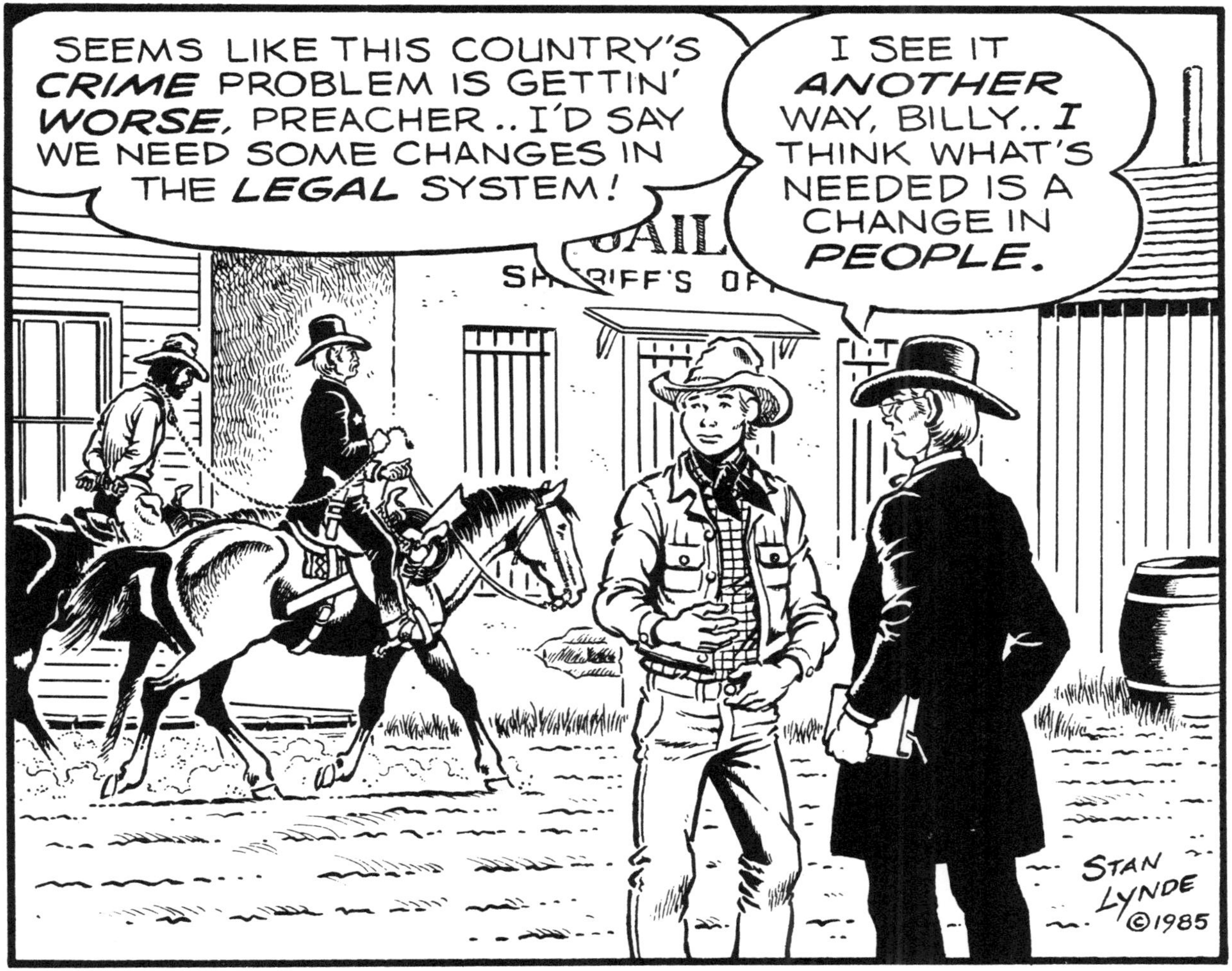
SEEMS LIKE THIS COUNTRY'S *CRIME* PROBLEM IS GETTIN' *WORSE,* PREACHER .. I'D SAY WE NEED SOME CHANGES IN THE *LEGAL* SYSTEM!
I SEE IT *ANOTHER* WAY, BILLY.. *I* THINK WHAT'S NEEDED IS A CHANGE IN *PEOPLE*.
STAN LYNDE ©1985

Age certainly does have an effect on the way we make use of our energy, and I'm always amazed at the way young hunters attack the world as if there were no limits to that valuable commodity.

For them, there *are* no limits; a few minutes rest and they're ready to go again, full speed ahead!

One day, while hunting near Columbus, Montana, a friend of my then teen-aged son decided he'd chase down a running deer..on *foot*. I pointed out to him that such a pursuit wouldn't be possible even for him, and that it was a waste of energy.

He really didn't know what I was talking about.

After a day's hunting that began well before sunrise, young hunters play racquetball or go to a dance.

Old hunters like me take a hot shower and turn up the electric blanket.

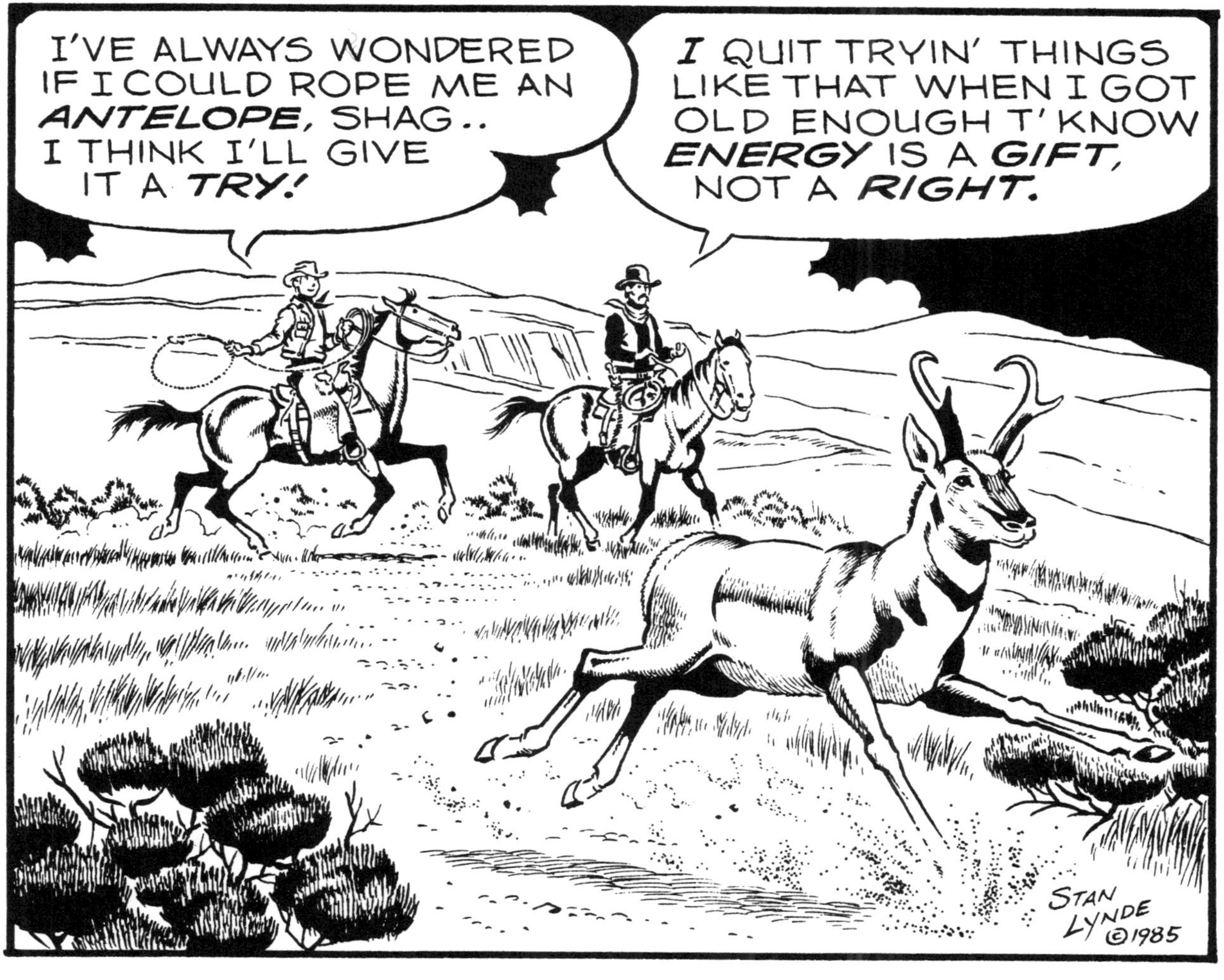
I'VE ALWAYS WONDERED IF I COULD ROPE ME AN ANTELOPE, SHAG.. I THINK I'LL GIVE IT A TRY!
I QUIT TRYIN' THINGS LIKE THAT WHEN I GOT OLD ENOUGH T' KNOW ENERGY IS A GIFT, NOT A RIGHT.
STAN LYNDE ©1985

To the person who loves his country, a traitor is hard indeed to understand. To enjoy the blessings of freedom and opportunity our nation grants its people and then to betray that nation for money seems inconceivable, but it has happened since our beginnings and no doubt will happen as long as our nation exists.

History seems to prove that there is no limit to the evil man is capable of, but individuals continue to arise who demonstrate there's no limit to the good we're capable of, either.

I like to believe that for every Josef Mengele, somewhere there's a Mother Theresa.

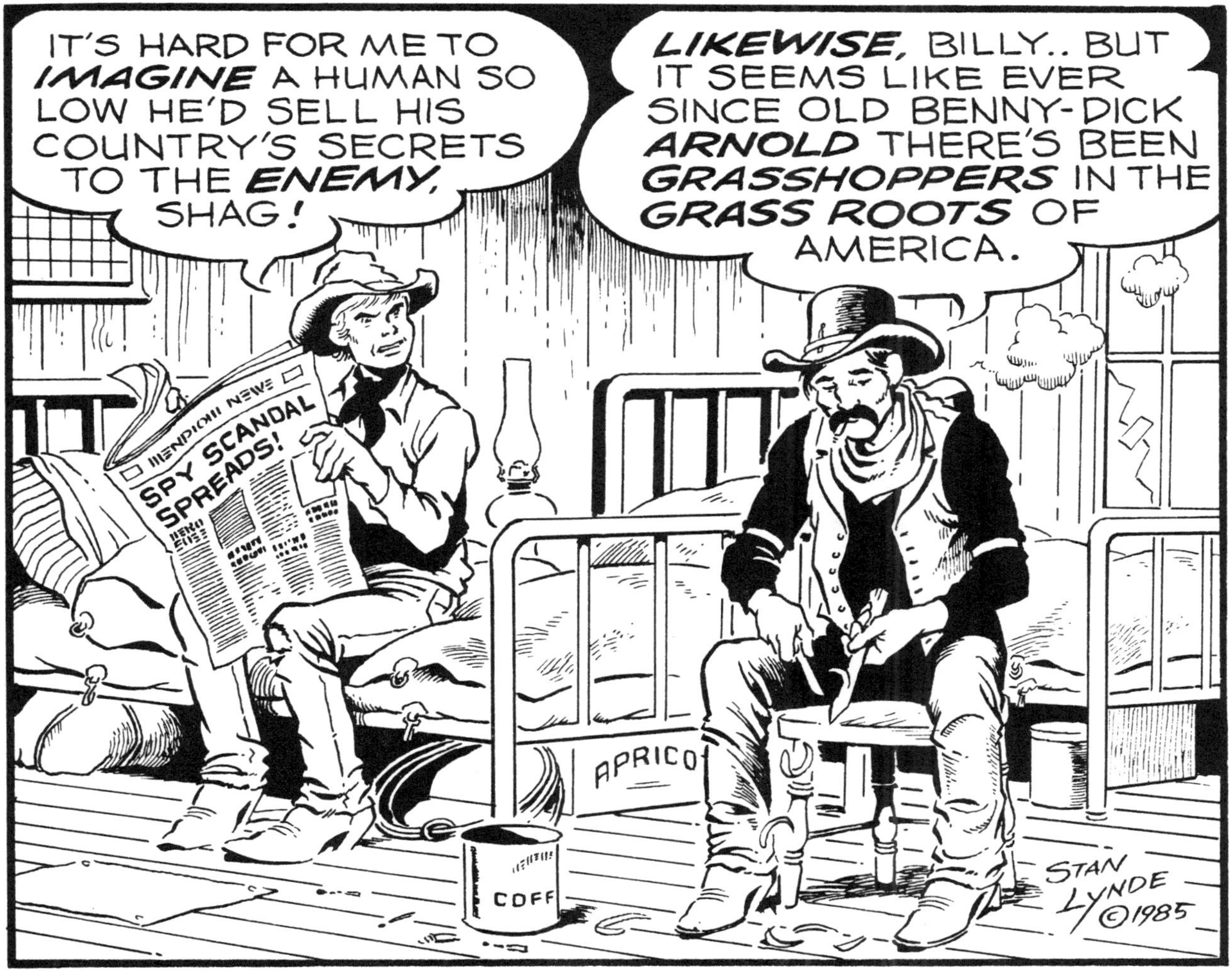
IT'S HARD FOR ME TO IMAGINE A HUMAN SO LOW HE'D SELL HIS COUNTRY'S SECRETS TO THE ENEMY, SHAG!
LIKEWISE, BILLY.. BUT IT SEEMS LIKE EVER SINCE OLD BENNY-DICK ARNOLD THERE'S BEEN GRASSHOPPERS IN THE GRASS ROOTS OF AMERICA.
SPY SCANDAL SPREADS!
APRICO
COFF
STAN LYNDE ©1985

Maybe it would be better if we could keep our emotions out of our decisions, but I don't think I know anyone who can.

For most of us, the reason we *make* decisions is the way we feel, and I think the best we can do is try to decide matters as much as we can, anyway, on the basis of the facts.

Perhaps a computer could be programmed for decision-making without emotion, but computers never seem to have much *fun*.

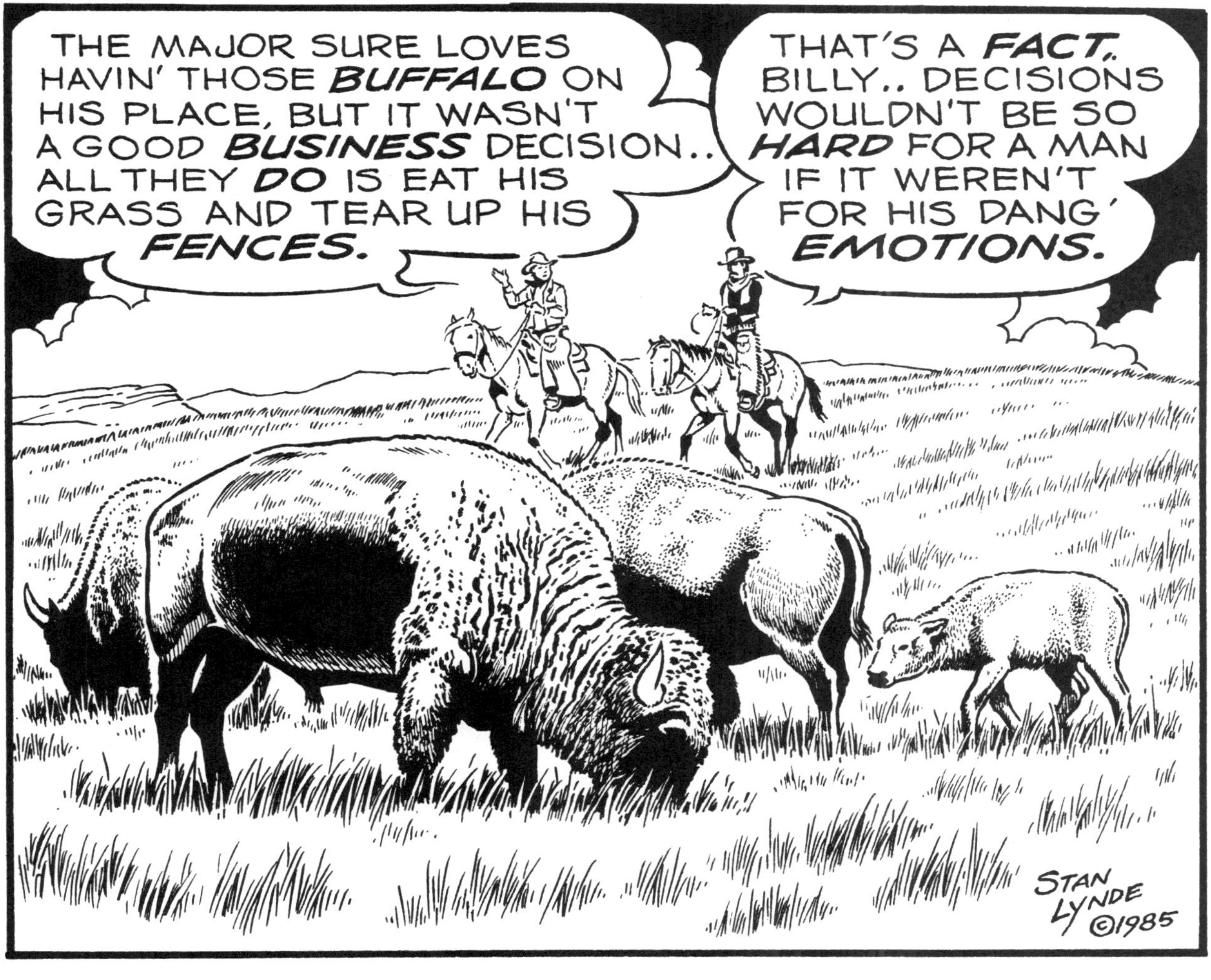
THE MAJOR SURE LOVES HAVIN' THOSE BUFFALO ON HIS PLACE, BUT IT WASN'T A GOOD BUSINESS DECISION.. ALL THEY DO IS EAT HIS GRASS AND TEAR UP HIS FENCES.
THAT'S A FACT, BILLY.. DECISIONS WOULDN'T BE SO HARD FOR A MAN IF IT WEREN'T FOR HIS DANG' EMOTIONS.
STAN LYNDE ©1985

There's the story of the man who went to the ticket counter of a major airline and asked the young woman on duty to sell him a ticket to Los Angeles, but send his luggage to Florida.

"But sir," she protested, "we can't do that!"

"Why not?" he replied, "you did it *last* time."

Kidding aside, I think the airlines do a pretty good job these days of delivering both passengers and luggage safely to the same destination. I've only had mine take separate trips four or five times, but I try to fly with a carry-on whenever possible.

Here at home the problem is under control. I'm here, and my luggage is over there in the closet.

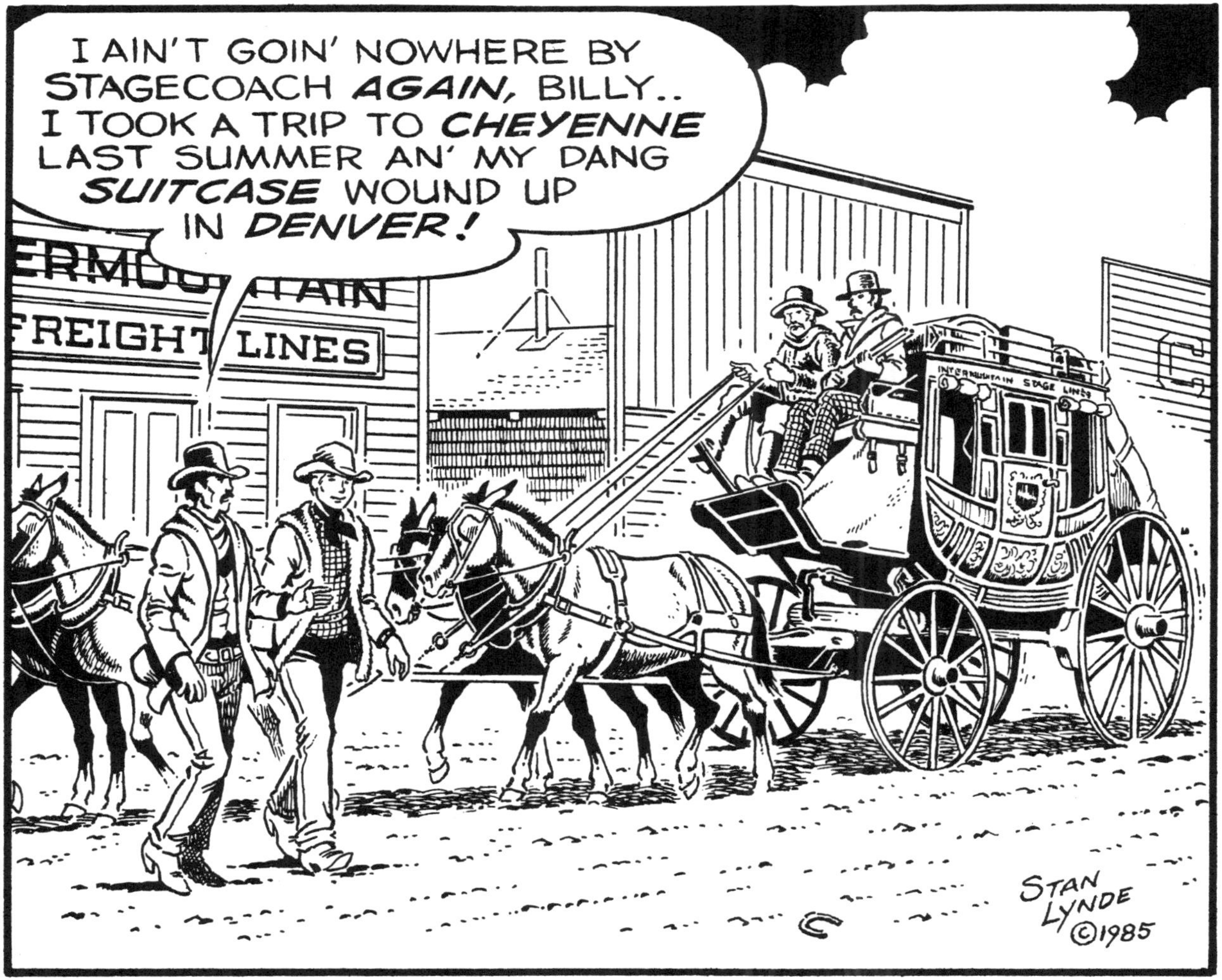
I AIN'T GOIN' NOWHERE BY STAGECOACH AGAIN, BILLY.. I TOOK A TRIP TO CHEYENNE LAST SUMMER AN' MY DANG SUITCASE WOUND UP IN DENVER!
ERMOUNTAIN FREIGHT LINES
STAN LYNDE ©1985

To the city dweller, weather is largely a matter of convenience and inconvenience, of wearing or not wearing a raincoat and carrying an umbrella, or of having to postpone the picnic.

But to the farmer and rancher weather is literally of life and death importance, and rainfall in a dry year can make the difference between economic survival and disaster.

It may well be that everybody talks about the weather and that nobody does anything about it, but in the rural west, at least, it's never taken for granted.

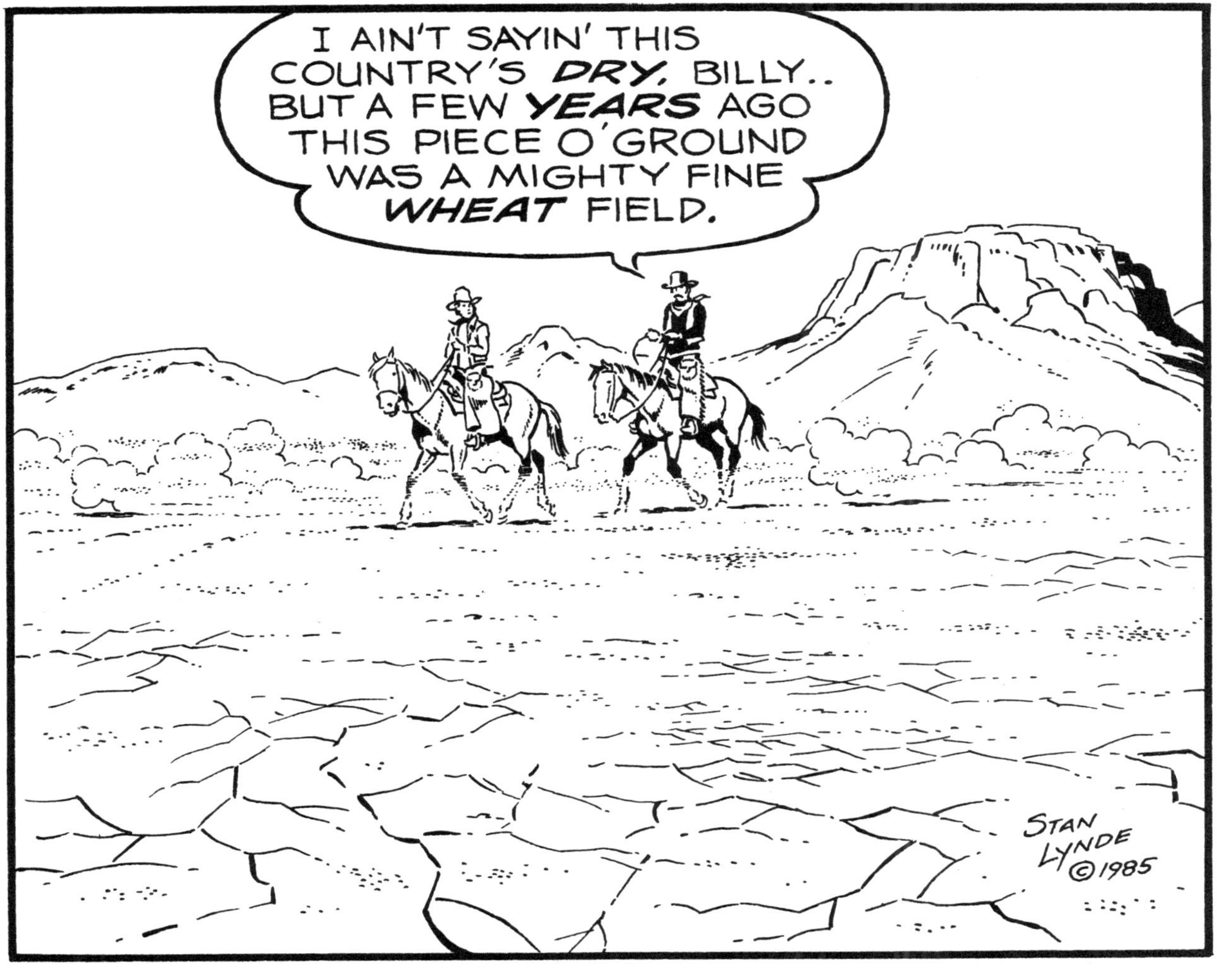
I AIN'T SAYIN' THIS COUNTRY'S DRY, BILLY.. BUT A FEW YEARS AGO THIS PIECE O'GROUND WAS A MIGHTY FINE WHEAT FIELD.
STAN LYNDE ©1985

Most of us finally get around to listening to what the preachers say only after we've tried everything else and our lives are so messed up we can't find anywhere else to turn.

At such a time, we may even be desperate enough to go to church, and a few of the *really* desperate may even change their lives.

Many such people then become quite happy and enthusiastic, and "Amazing Grace" gets to be number one on their personal hit parade.

His grace *is* amazing, but it's also pretty amazing how long it takes some of us to *accept* it.

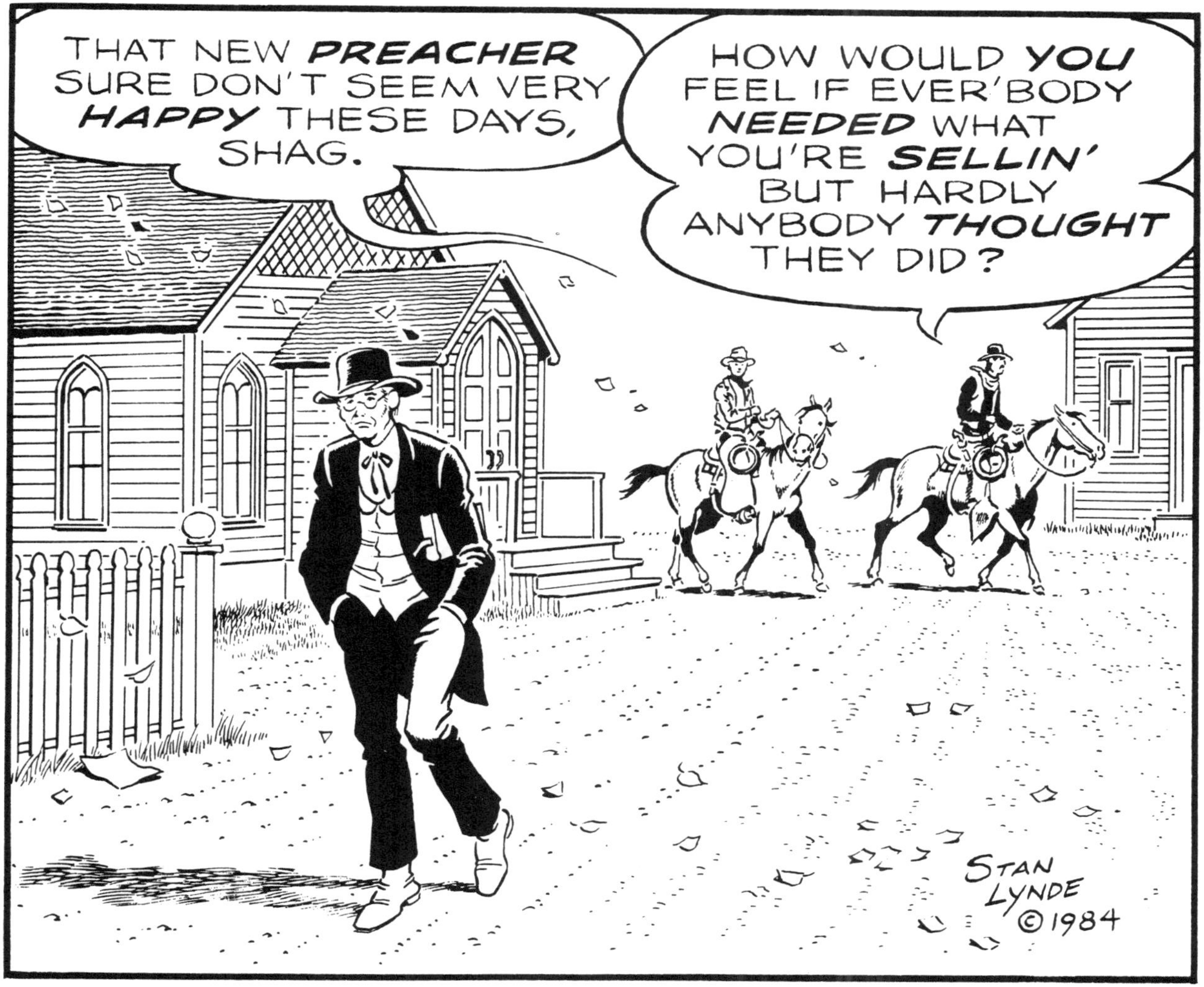
THAT NEW **PREACHER** SURE DON'T SEEM VERY **HAPPY** THESE DAYS, SHAG.
HOW WOULD **YOU** FEEL IF EVER'BODY **NEEDED** WHAT YOU'RE **SELLIN'** BUT HARDLY ANYBODY **THOUGHT** THEY DID?
STAN LYNDE ©1984

This past year, here in the Flathead Valley, we've seen bear, fox, deer, and a mountain lion--all just a matter of yards from our house.

Animals aren't so dumb; they've learned that where people herd together and build their nests is where the *food* is, so many of them mosey on down from the mountains and stock up, especially in a dry year.

It's only fair, I guess. We keep moving deeper into *their* turf with our cross-country skis, snowshoes, hiking boots, trail bikes, snowmobiles, tents, campers, cabins, summer homes, rifles, and boats, so I guess we shouldn't be surprised if they move into *our* space.

We're just trying to have a good time.

They're just trying to *survive*.

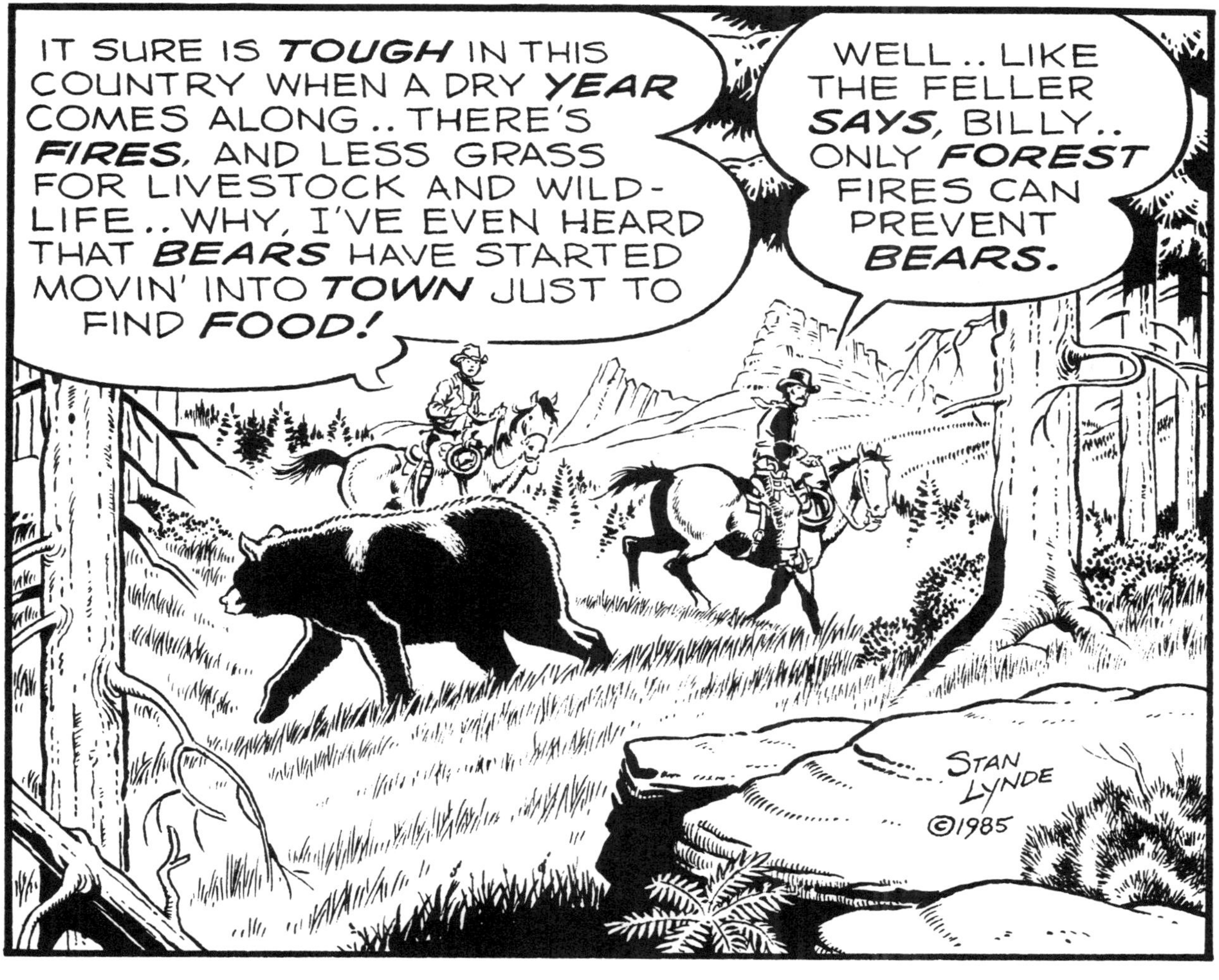
IT SURE IS TOUGH IN THIS COUNTRY WHEN A DRY YEAR COMES ALONG.. THERE'S FIRES, AND LESS GRASS FOR LIVESTOCK AND WILD-LIFE.. WHY, I'VE EVEN HEARD THAT BEARS HAVE STARTED MOVIN' INTO TOWN JUST TO FIND FOOD!
WELL.. LIKE THE FELLER SAYS, BILLY.. ONLY FOREST FIRES CAN PREVENT BEARS.
STAN LYNDE ©1985

Finding a place to hunt these days is becoming almost as important as finding the game, and it's getting tougher.

Not only are landowners getting a bit tired of having Bossy and Old Dobbin snuffed by trigger-happy Nimrods who can't tell a pronghorn from a pumpkin, they're not too crazy about having their gates left open or their water-tanks ventilated, either.

I was caught in a cross-fire once in the Gravelly Mountains when two groups of orange-clad bipeds opened up on a covey of cow elk and calves who were unwise enough to stroll between their lines. Unfortunately, I was near the wapiti ladies and their kids at the time, and I suddenly developed a passionate desire to be *smaller*.

I hit the dirt, and quivered there in prayer and meditation while the fusillade passed through, and cut branches from, a big pine tree overhead. I'd have become even *more* intimate with the earth, except that-- like the Bill Mauldin cartoon--my *buttons* were in the way.

At any rate, the elk and I both somehow escaped injury, and I assume the "hunters" did, too. If they did, I'm glad, but I'm still not sorry about all those things I *called* them. Mark Twain said it best, as usual:

"I cannot escape the conclusion that in certain desperate and tryin' circumstances, profanity provides a release denied even to prayer."

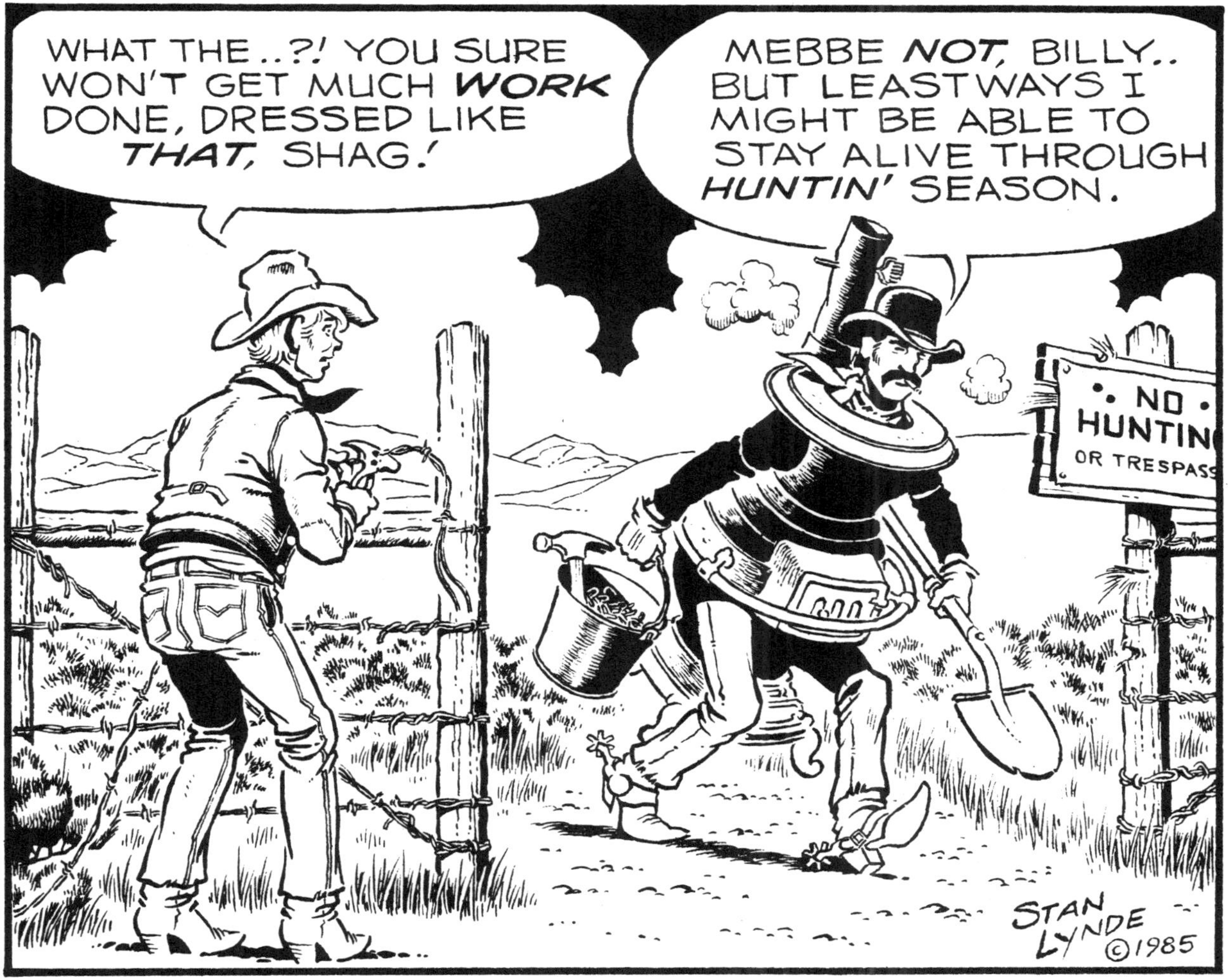
WHAT THE..?! YOU SURE WON'T GET MUCH **WORK** DONE, DRESSED LIKE ***THAT,*** SHAG.!
MEBBE ***NOT,*** BILLY.. BUT LEASTWAYS I MIGHT BE ABLE TO STAY ALIVE THROUGH ***HUNTIN'*** SEASON.
NO HUNTIN
OR TRESPASS
STAN LYNDE ©1985

Is the office-seeker really sincere when he makes all those promises? Or does he think we don't remember the ones he made during his *last* campaign?

I'll give him the benefit of the doubt; I think he's sincere enough, but he's so full of hope and ambition at such a time that he tends to turn his "I want tos" into "I wills."

I think that's the way we should *hear* him, too; all things may, after all, be possible.

It's just that most of them aren't very *likely*.

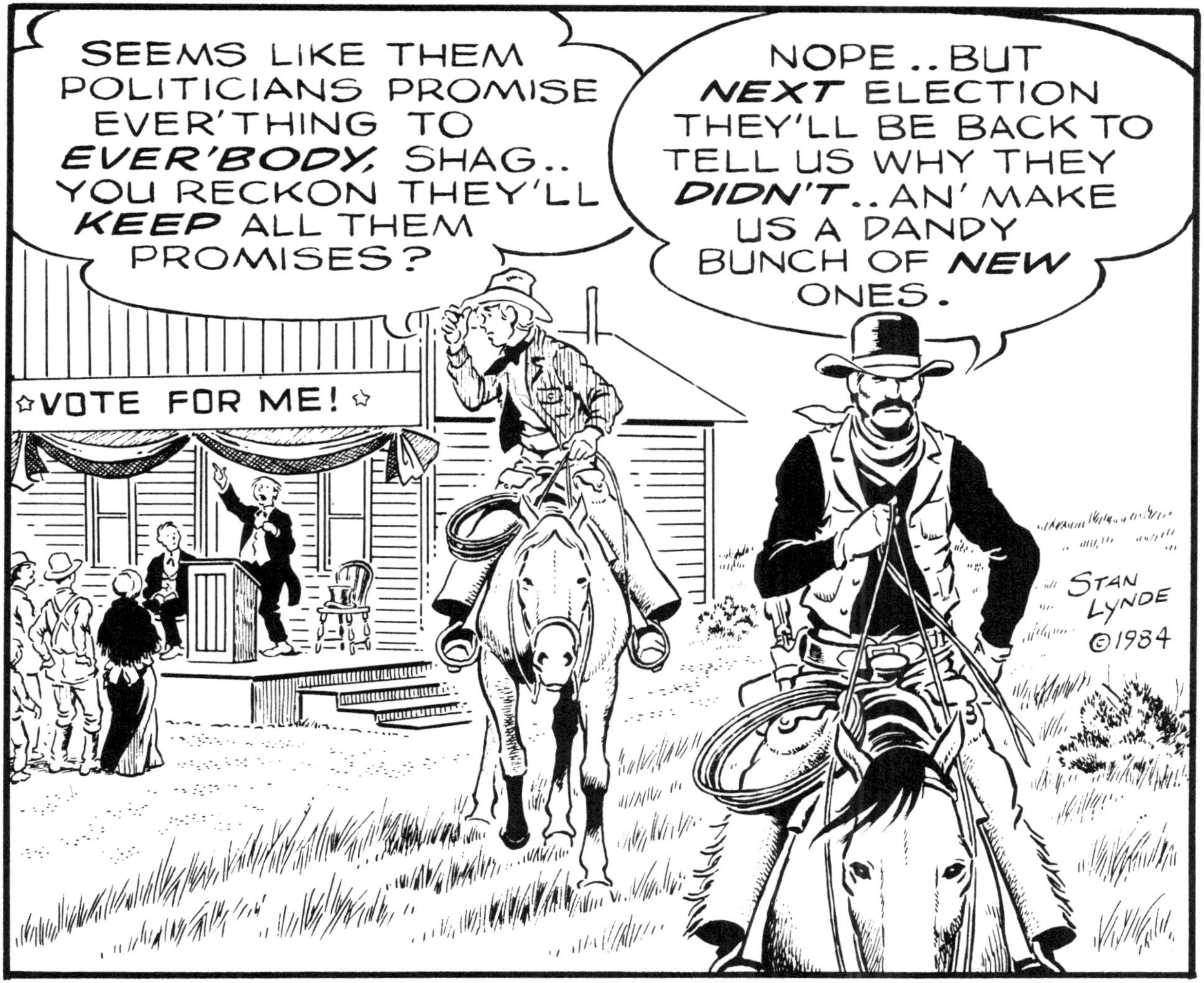
SEEMS LIKE THEM POLITICIANS PROMISE EVER'THING TO EVER'BODY, SHAG.. YOU RECKON THEY'LL KEEP ALL THEM PROMISES?
NOPE ..BUT NEXT ELECTION THEY'LL BE BACK TO TELL US WHY THEY DIDN'T..AN' MAKE US A DANDY BUNCH OF NEW ONES.
VOTE FOR ME!
STAN LYNDE ©1984

I guess it's only human to become attached to the things we own and love. I've known men who have replaced or rebuilt everything on their old truck except the ashtray who proudly tell you they've had their rig since 1946 and it still runs like a fine Swiss watch.

Well, it *ought* to. If medical science ever gets all the bugs out of the *transplant* business, so can we *all*.

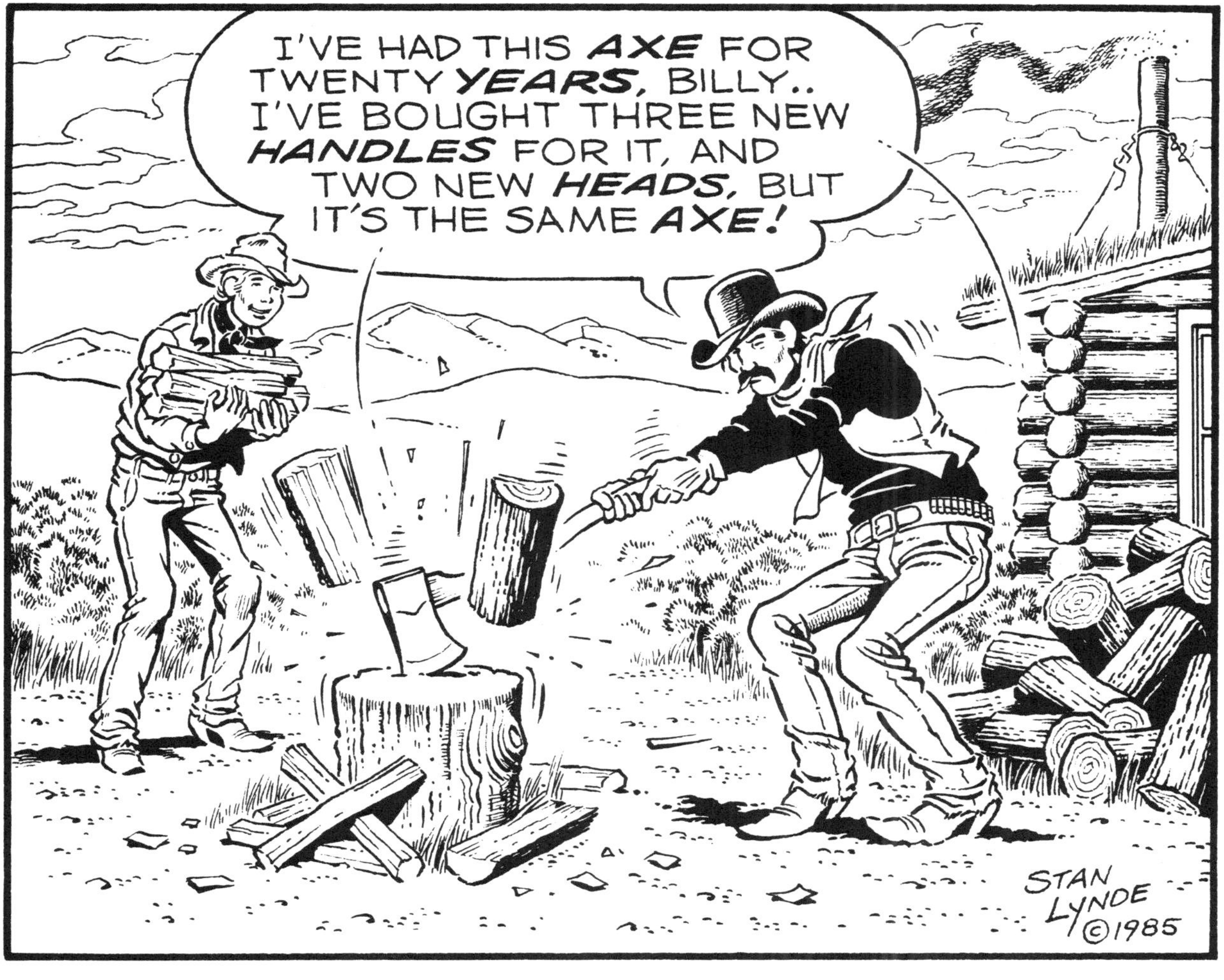
I'VE HAD THIS AXE FOR TWENTY YEARS, BILLY.. I'VE BOUGHT THREE NEW HANDLES FOR IT, AND TWO NEW HEADS, BUT IT'S THE SAME AXE!
STAN LYNDE ©1985

Pity the poor politician. If he tells us the whole truth, including the bad news, while his opponent tells us only the *good* news (and what we want to hear) his career may be in deep trouble.

Maybe we should all think about that when we complain about the office-holder; it is an old truth that in America we usually get just about the kind of government we *deserve*.

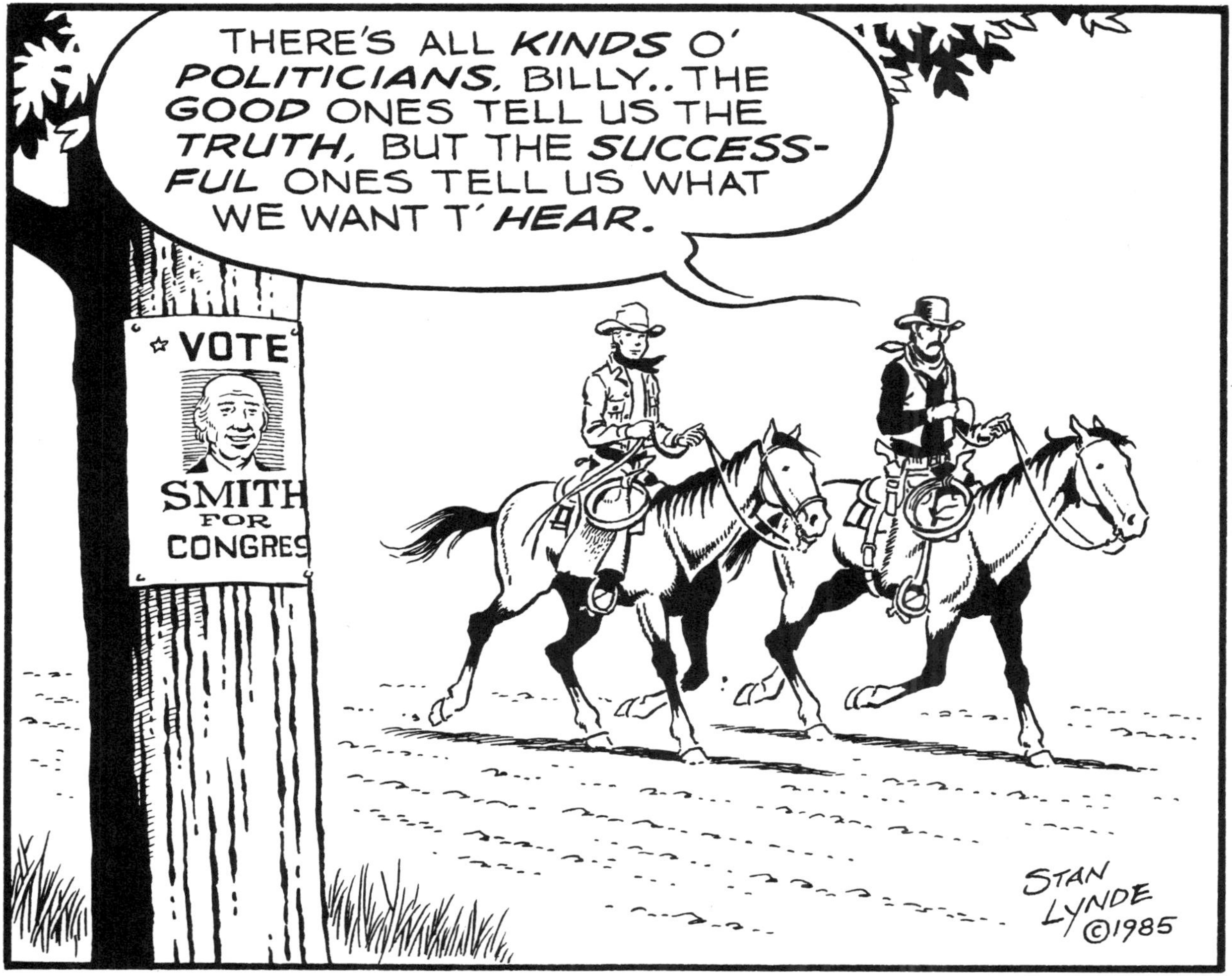
THERE'S ALL KINDS O' POLITICIANS, BILLY.. THE GOOD ONES TELL US THE TRUTH, BUT THE SUCCESS-FUL ONES TELL US WHAT WE WANT T' HEAR.
VOTE
SMITH
FOR
CONGRES
STAN LYNDE ©1985

I know a man who claims he understands women; his divorce becomes final this week.

Just kidding--I don't *really* know such a man, and if one should make such a claim within my hearing I wouldn't believe him anyway. Oh, I'm familiar with the modern notion that men and women are equal and the same in all respects, I just don't happen to believe it. Equal, certainly; the same, never.

I believe the creator made male and female different as part of His grand design, and that while the sexes my know each other, neither can fully *understand* the other. To me, that's part of the beauty of His plan; our differences can also be our strengths, and a marriage can become a stronger unit than any individual.

Understanding isn't necessary; love and commitment *are*.

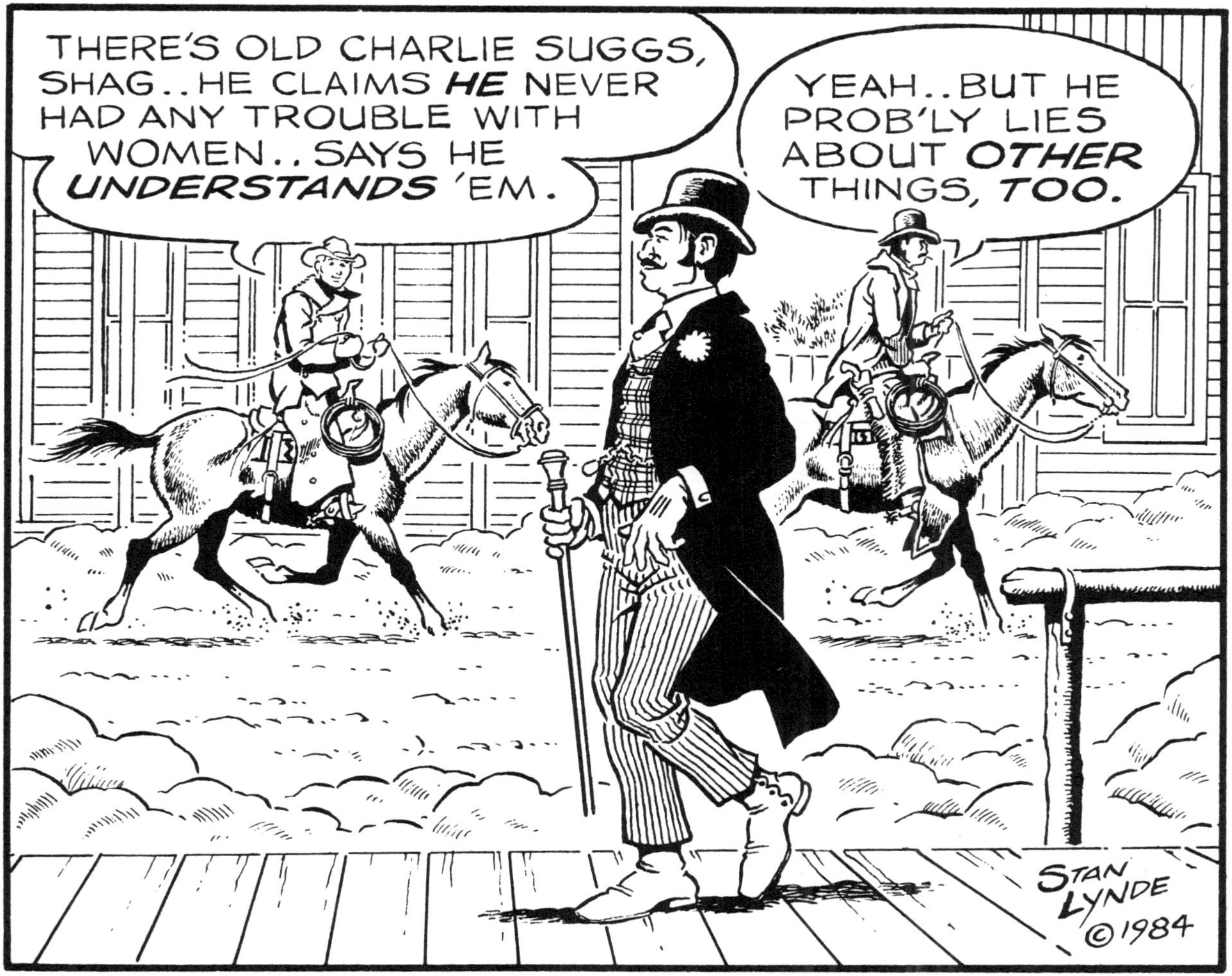
THERE'S OLD CHARLIE SUGGS, SHAG..HE CLAIMS HE NEVER HAD ANY TROUBLE WITH WOMEN..SAYS HE UNDERSTANDS 'EM.
YEAH..BUT HE PROB'LY LIES ABOUT OTHER THINGS, TOO.
STAN LYNDE ©1984

Unlicensed, free-roaming dogs can be a major problem in a small town-- even a menace. They freely forage amid the trash cans, litter the alleys, decorate the neighbor's lawn, multiply like mad, and they sometimes even carry rabies.

Most towns have licensing and leash laws, but they're like *all* laws in that only the law-abiding and well-behaved pooches wear licenses and leashes; the renegade hounds just keep on doing whatever they please.

One of the lesser-known facts about the celebrated Wild Bill Hickok is that while town marshal of Abilene, Kansas, the long-haired gunfighter was paid 50 cents a head by the town fathers for each unlicensed dog he shot within the city limits.

Sometimes, the way of the outlaw is hard.

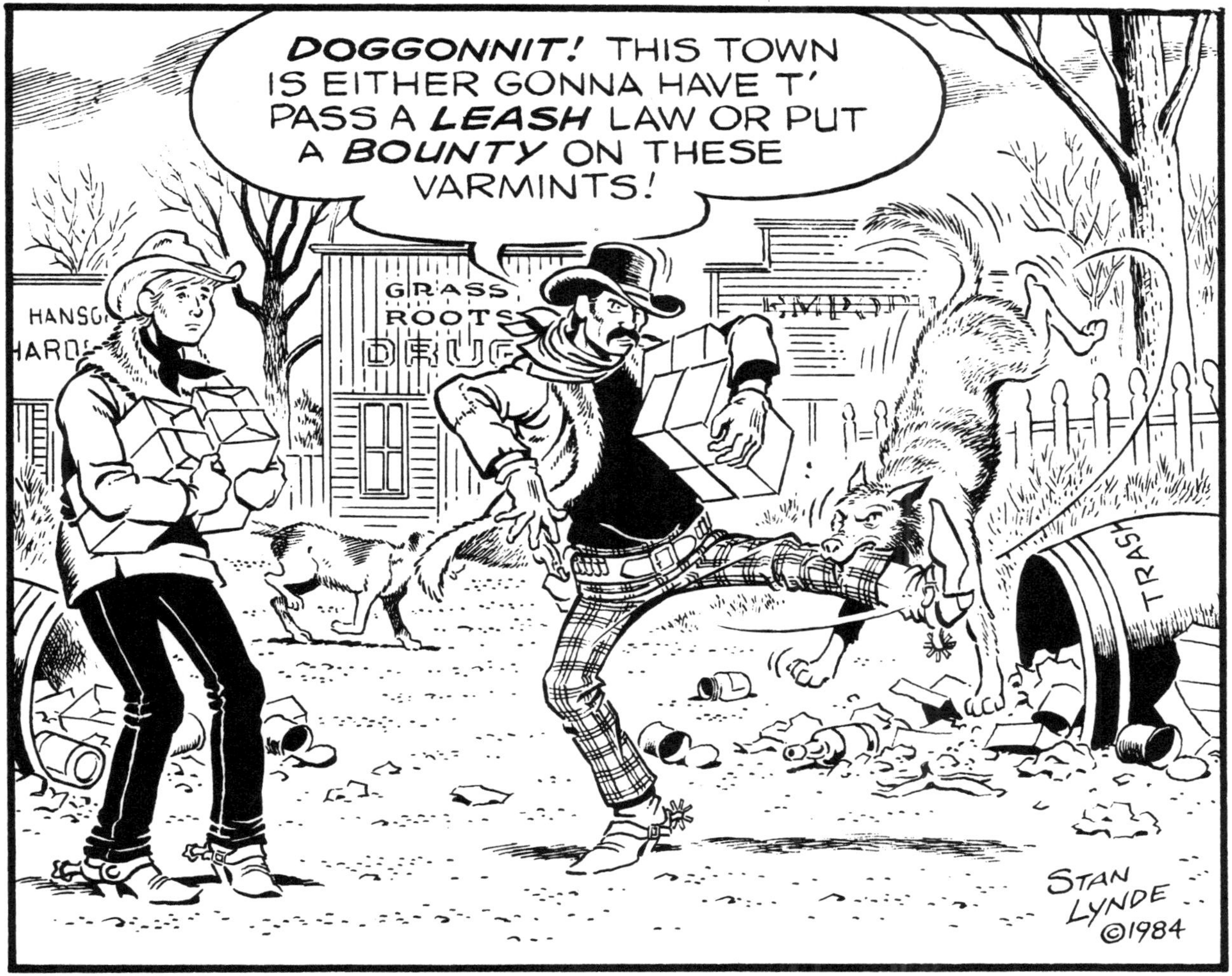
DOGGONNIT! THIS TOWN IS EITHER GONNA HAVE T' PASS A LEASH LAW OR PUT A BOUNTY ON THESE VARMINTS!
HANSO
HARD
GRASS ROOTS DRUG
TRASH
STAN LYNDE ©1984

When both sheep and cattle shared the open range, prejudice ruled the day, and in some cases even led to shooting wars.

Having killed off or pushed off the buffalo and Indians who formerly occupied the grasslands, the cattleman claimed the grazing land as his own. Being assured by the government that the land was public land, so did the sheepman--he certainly was part of the public, and felt he had the same right to practice free enterprise as the cattleman.

Cattlemen claimed sheep smelled bad and ruined waterholes. They claimed sheep ruined the range by overgrazing.

Well, sheep *do* smell bad, but nobody ever confused the fine aroma of the average steer with that of mountain flowers in July, *either*. And sheep *do* overgraze the range if confined too long in one area. So do *cattle*.

Prejudice seems to be made up of ignorance, fear, greed, and the human trait of wanting to feel superior to somebody.

It's *not* one of our better traits.

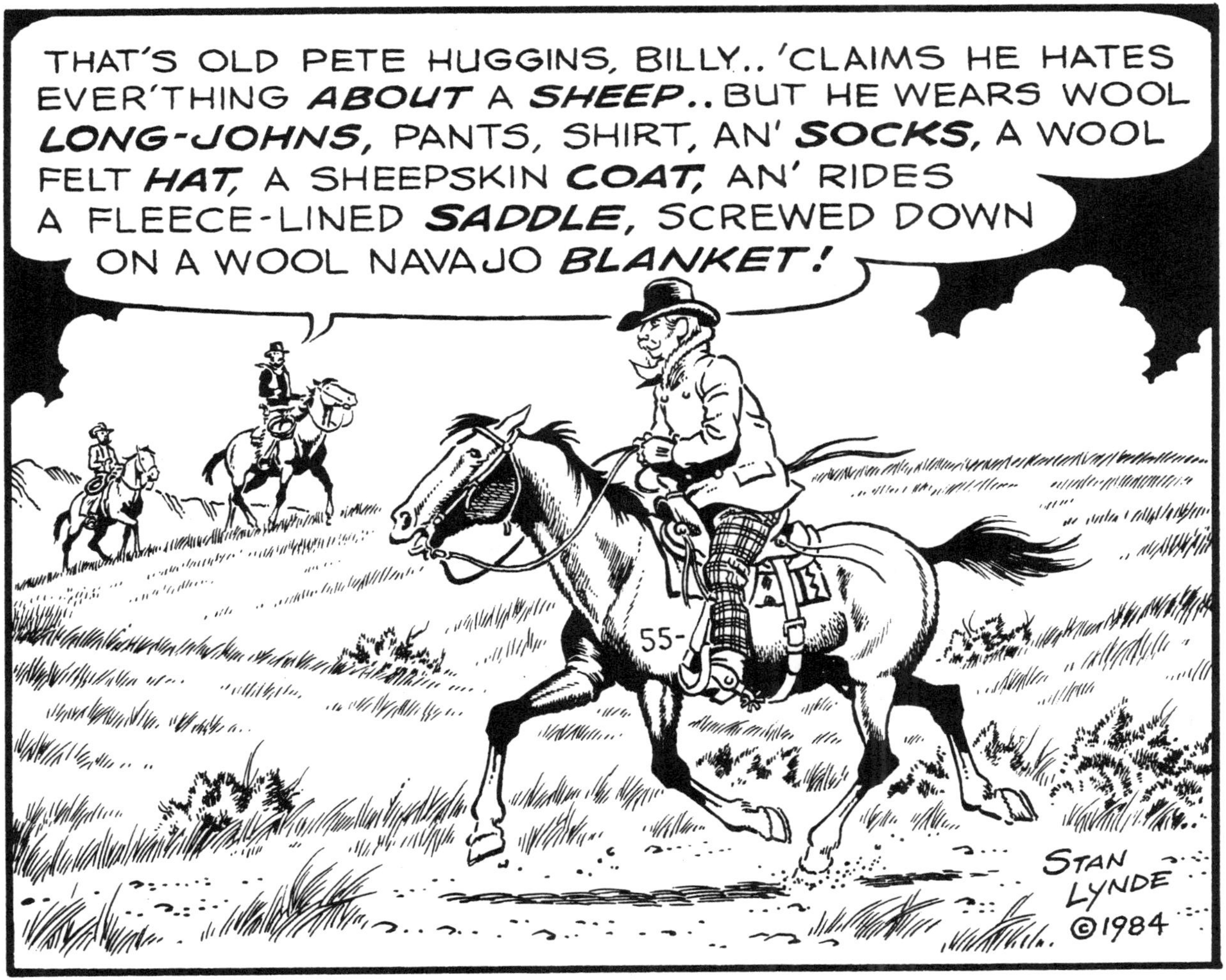
THAT'S OLD PETE HUGGINS, BILLY.. 'CLAIMS HE HATES EVER'THING ABOUT A SHEEP.. BUT HE WEARS WOOL LONG-JOHNS, PANTS, SHIRT, AN' SOCKS, A WOOL FELT HAT, A SHEEPSKIN COAT, AN' RIDES A FLEECE-LINED SADDLE, SCREWED DOWN ON A WOOL NAVAJO BLANKET!
55-
STAN LYNDE ©1984

According to the cowboy's proud code, a rider neither grabbed for the saddle horn nor stepped off the hurricane deck of a horse who "swallered his head and went to buckin'"--he "hung and rattled" until thrown.

And if self-preservation got the better of him and he *did* step off, he'd better come up with a *very* good reason.

Shag has done just that; he's found a way to explain his departure from the horse--and the cowboy code--and still maintain his pride.

Discretion may well be the better part of valor, but it helps to have a good explanation handy.

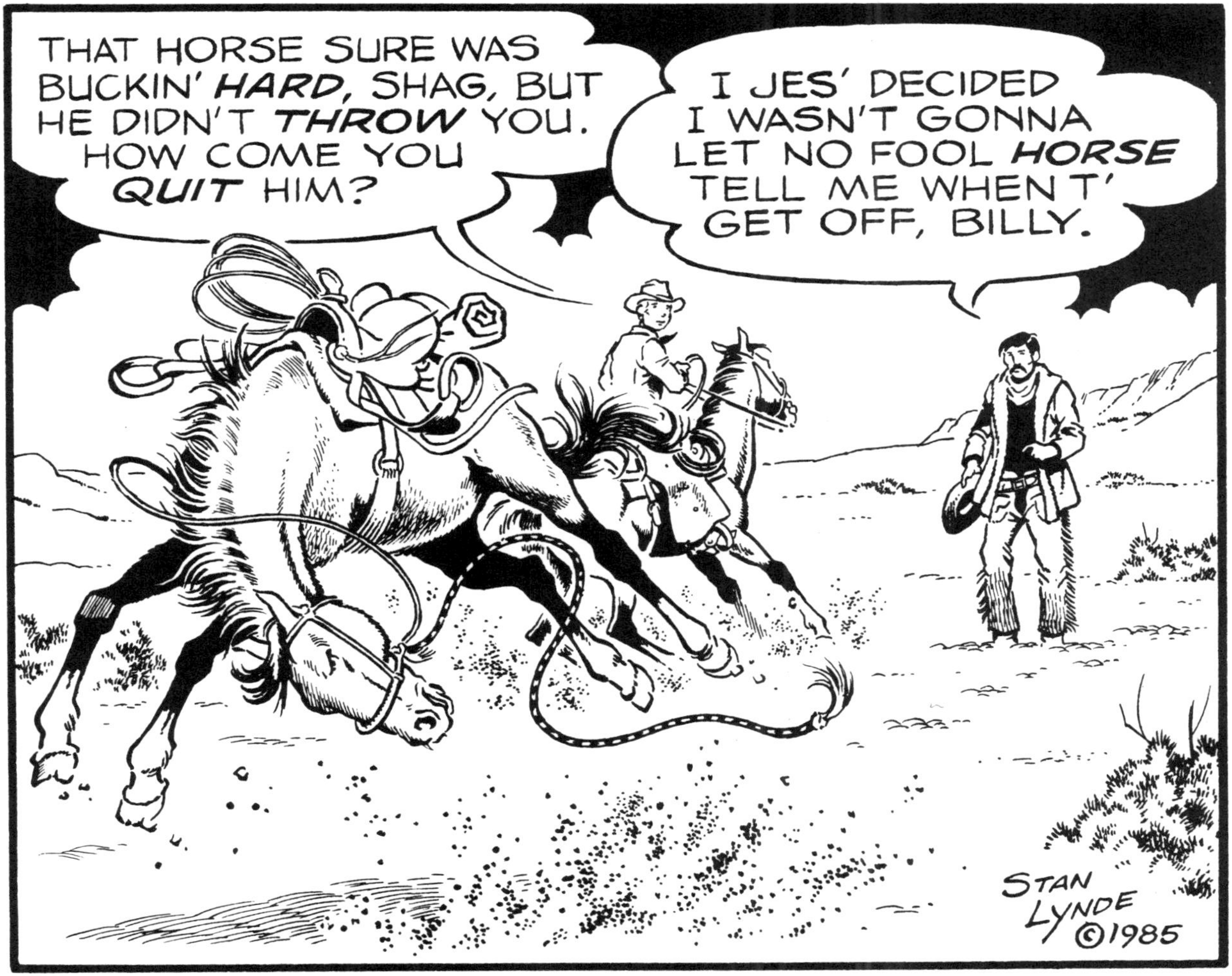
THAT HORSE SURE WAS BUCKIN' HARD, SHAG, BUT HE DIDN'T THROW YOU. HOW COME YOU QUIT HIM?
I JES' DECIDED I WASN'T GONNA LET NO FOOL HORSE TELL ME WHEN T' GET OFF, BILLY.
STAN LYNDE ©1985

Thanksgiving is a special day that has been set aside for being thankful, and I think that's fine as far as it goes.

First of all, the very word "thanksgiving" implies gratitude to something outside ourselves, which makes the whole thing just a little tough on the atheist. But then I suppose he can always thank his lucky stars, himself, or something.

I believe it's easier for all of us to concentrate on the problems and needs of our lives, sometimes to the point that we fail to recognize the many good things that are present all the time.

It's a good thing to set aside a day every year for the purpose of giving thanks.

It's even better to set aside some time for it every *day*.

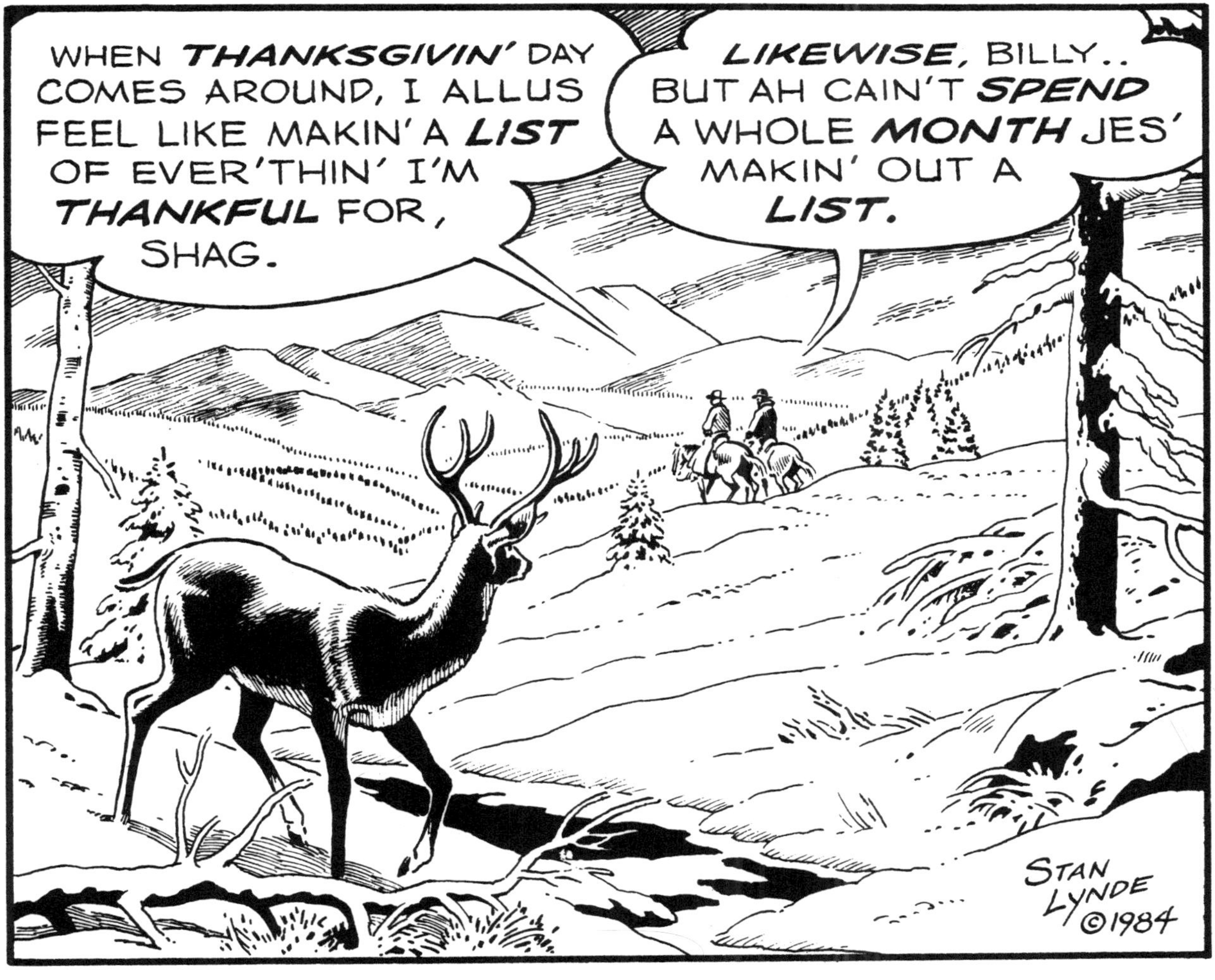
WHEN THANKSGIVIN' DAY COMES AROUND, I ALLUS FEEL LIKE MAKIN' A LIST OF EVER'THIN' I'M THANKFUL FOR, SHAG.
LIKEWISE, BILLY.. BUT AH CAIN'T SPEND A WHOLE MONTH JES' MAKIN' OUT A LIST.
STAN LYNDE ©1984

Rules should be impartial; they should apply equally to everyone.

Shag feels the game will go better if all the players have a roughly equal chance at winning, and for him this means that no player should have more cards than another. In the spirit of sportsmanship he's helping Mr. Tinhorn to prepare for an honest game.

The sheriff really doesn't object so much to Shag's intentions as he does to his method.

Poker was never *meant* to be a *contact* sport.

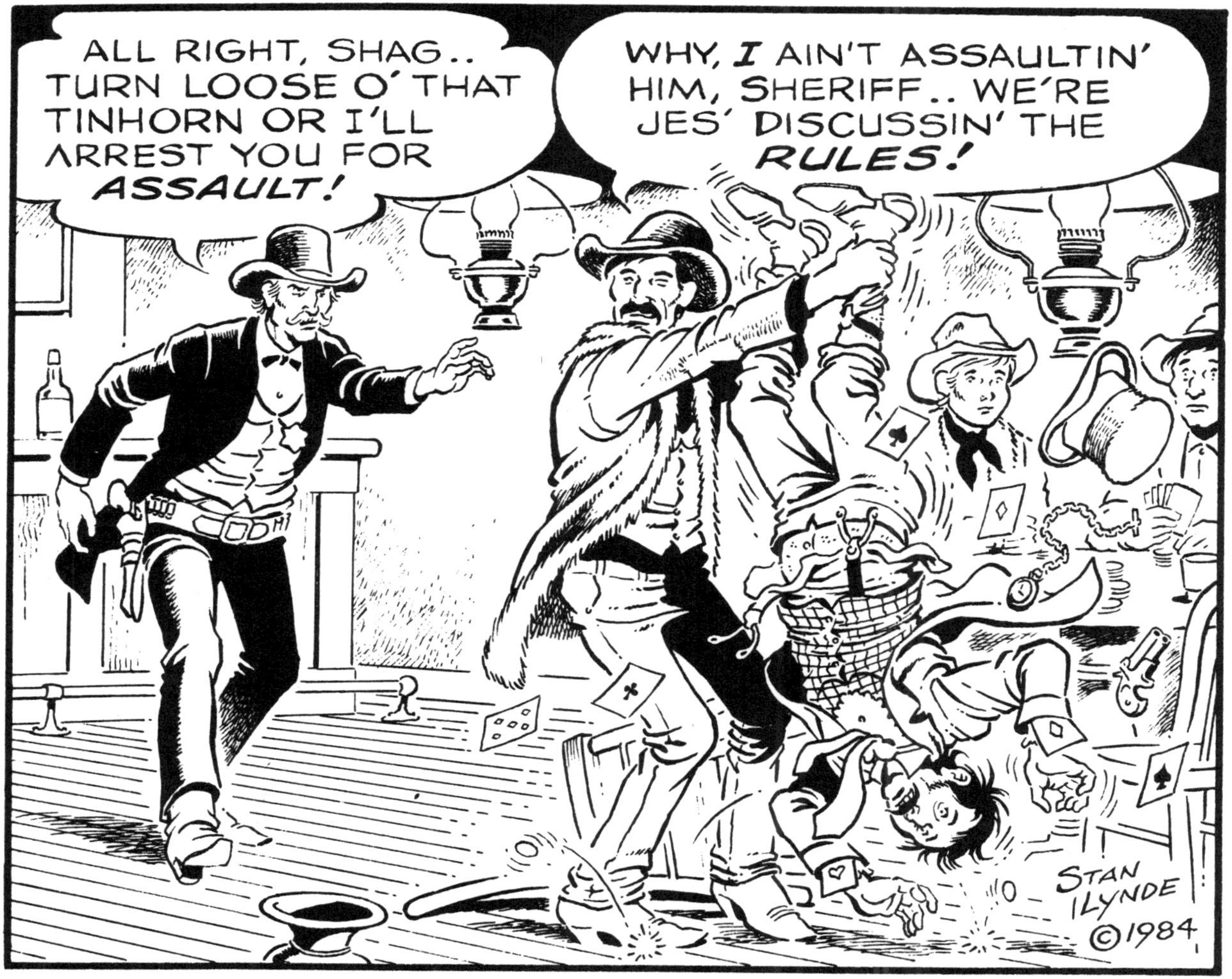
ALL RIGHT, SHAG.. TURN LOOSE O' THAT TINHORN OR I'LL ARREST YOU FOR ASSAULT!
WHY, I AIN'T ASSAULTIN' HIM, SHERIFF.. WE'RE JES' DISCUSSIN' THE RULES!
STAN LYNDE ©1984

Tell an avid hunter you think hunting is cruel, and you may very well learn more than you wanted to know about the alternative deaths an animal faces in the natural.

Done responsibly and well, I've found that hunting can be one of the finest experiences in life, providing its participants with special memories of golden days spent out-of-doors, of good friends, sunrises, sunsets, autumn leaves, and campfires--and an awareness of nature's beauty and order.

Done *irresponsibly,* it can be just as cruel as its critics think it is.

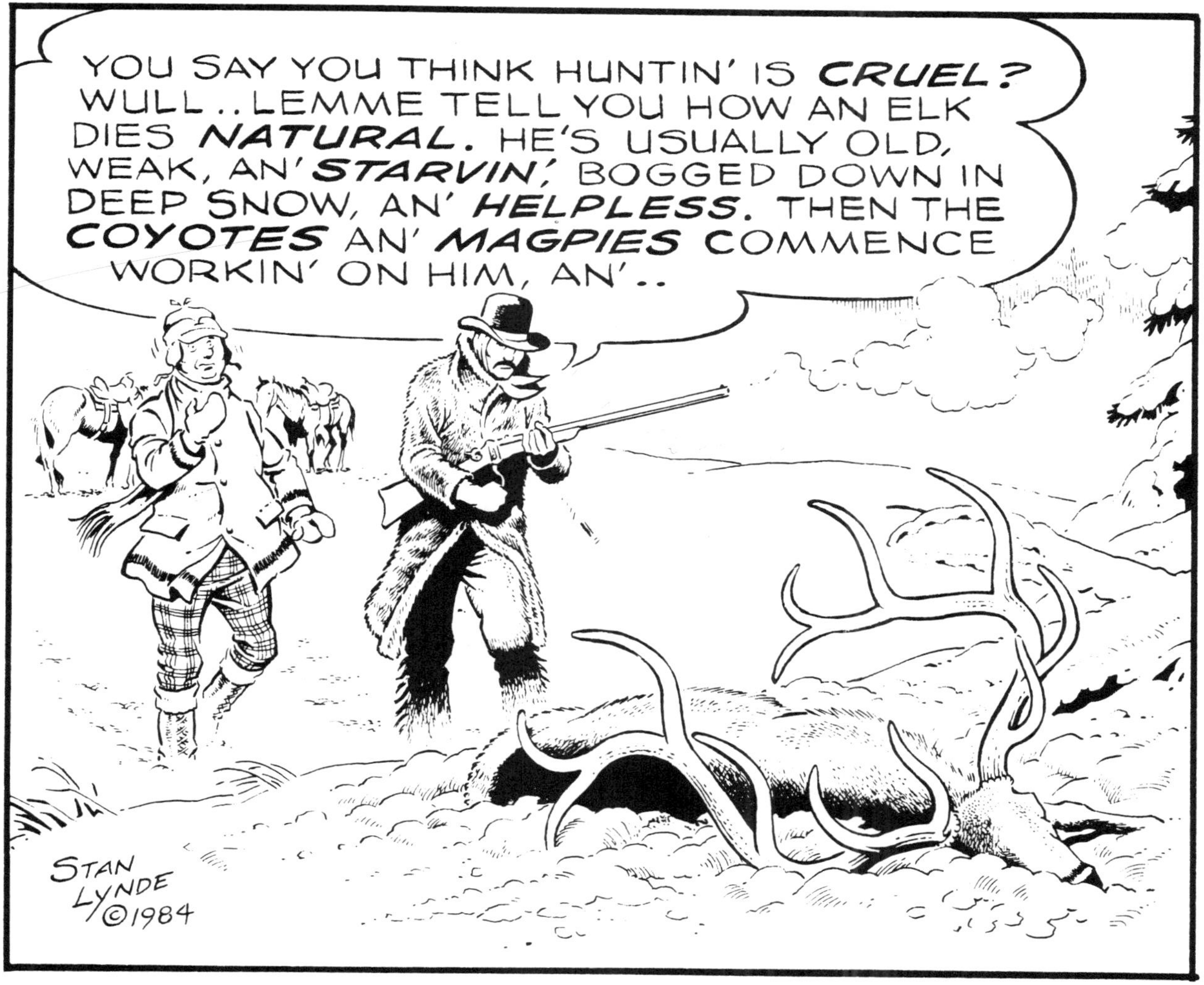
YOU SAY YOU THINK HUNTIN' IS CRUEL? WULL..LEMME TELL YOU HOW AN ELK DIES NATURAL. HE'S USUALLY OLD, WEAK, AN' STARVIN,' BOGGED DOWN IN DEEP SNOW, AN' HELPLESS. THEN THE COYOTES AN' MAGPIES COMMENCE WORKIN' ON HIM, AN'..
STAN LYNDE ©1984

Here in northern Montana, we've been having what the old-timers refer to as "a spell of weather."

For nearly a month now, the temperature has been below freezing, and for the past week it has remained stubbornly in the sub-zero range.

Surprisingly, we all seem to adapt; we've gone--quickly, it seems--from complaint to acceptance, and business as usual. And it's also surprising how the slightest move upward on the thermometer brings relief, and even comfort. It's up to three *above* this morning, and as soon as I can find my shorts and sandals I'll be ready for the *picnic*.

As for Shag, he's still in the complaint mode, but he has found a practical solution--he's learned that weather, and our perception of it--is a matter of *degree*.

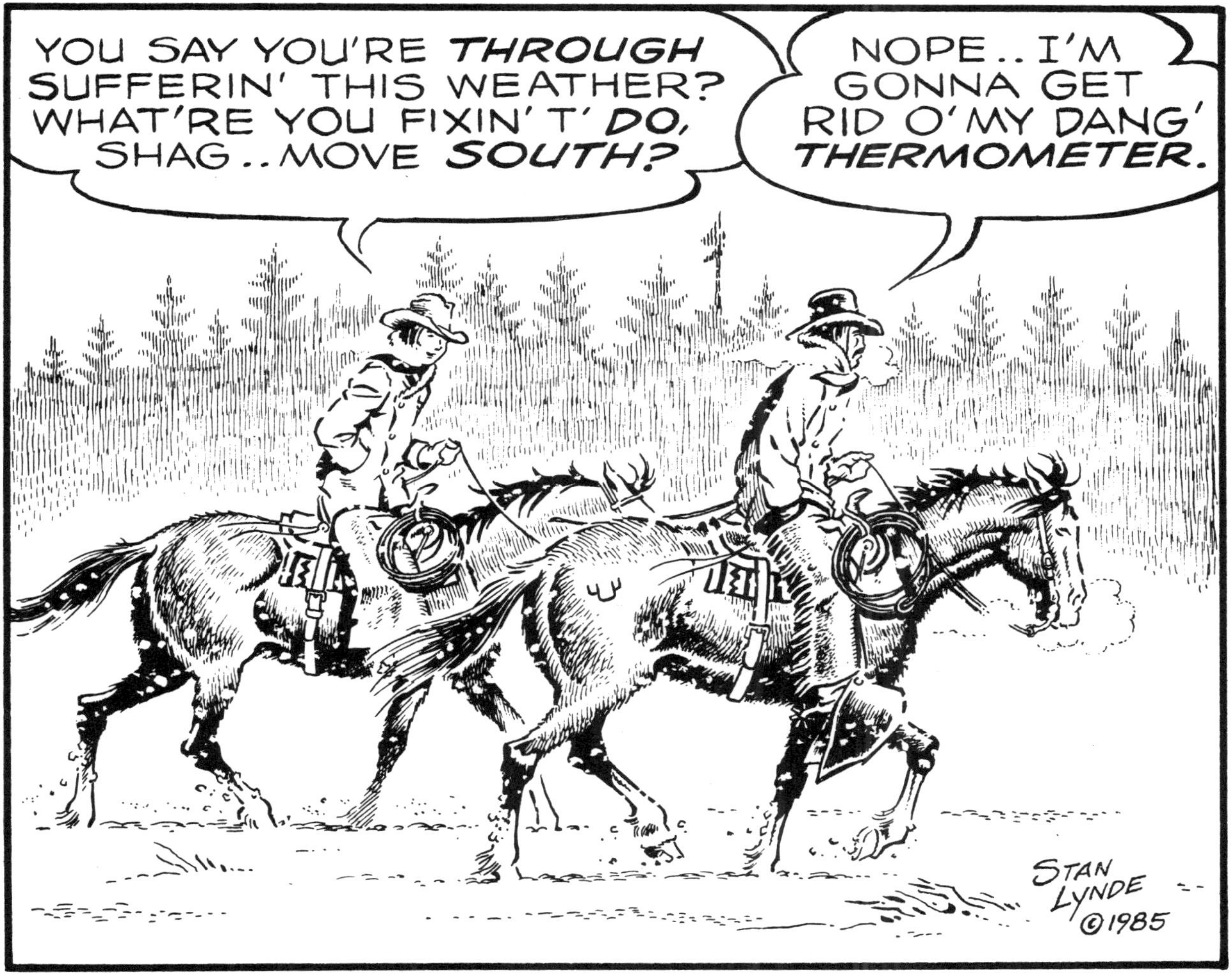
YOU SAY YOU'RE *THROUGH* SUFFERIN' THIS WEATHER? WHAT'RE YOU FIXIN' T' *DO*, SHAG..MOVE *SOUTH?*
NOPE..I'M GONNA GET RID O'MY DANG' *THERMOMETER*.
STAN LYNDE ©1985

Snow comes early in the mountains and stays late.

I remember an April in Red Lodge, Montana, when 77 inches of snow fell in a single storm.

Now we're used to snow here in Montana, even when it keeps falling well into June, but receiving over six feet on the level, with drifts as deep as 15 feet, is a bit unusual even for us.

I like snow, and I enjoy it.

But sometimes I find I've enjoyed about all of it I can *stand*.

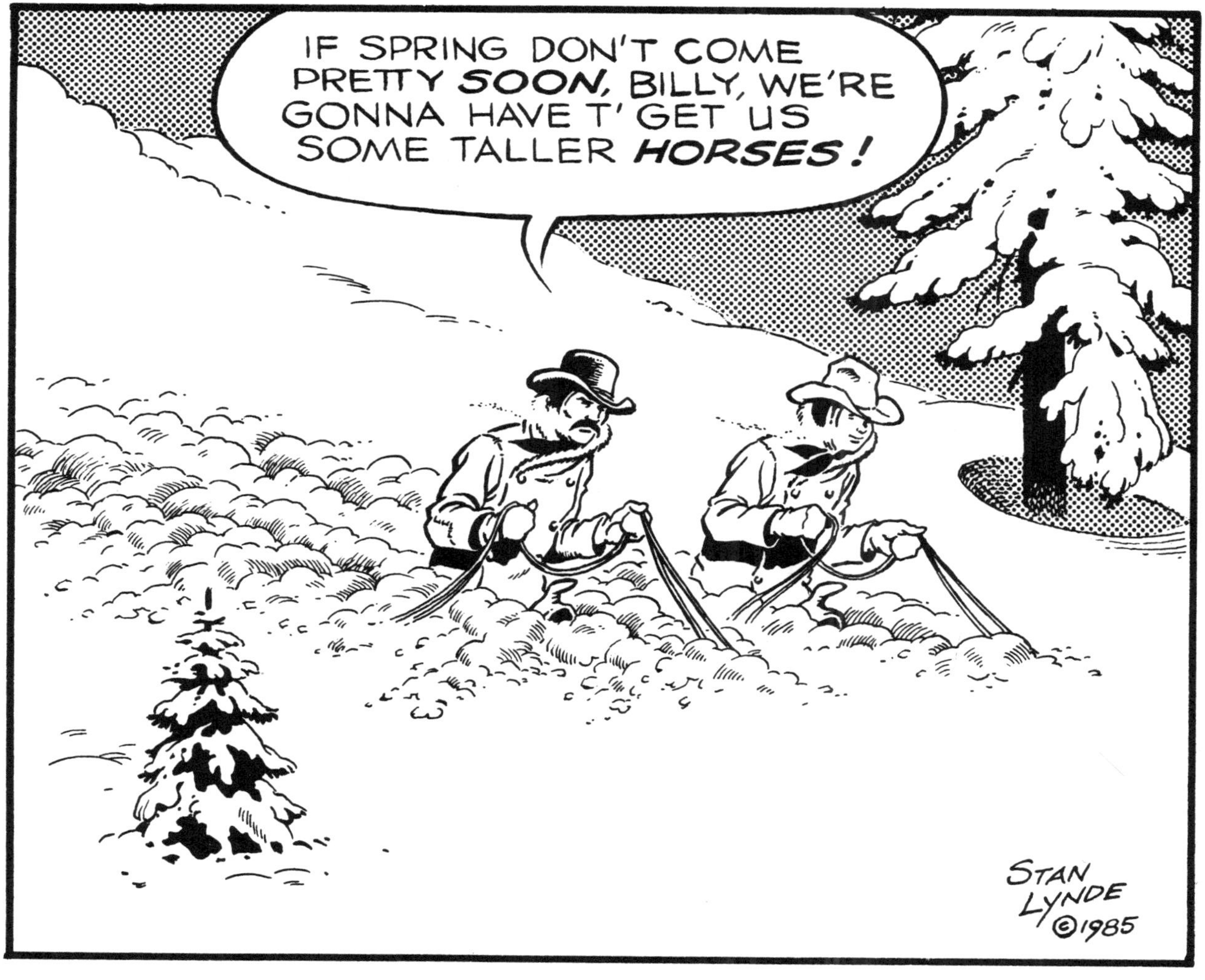
IF SPRING DON'T COME PRETTY SOON, BILLY, WE'RE GONNA HAVE T' GET US SOME TALLER HORSES!
STAN LYNDE ©1985

I've always considered the stockman to be a sort of apprentice to the Creator, who cares for his livestock as God cares for us.

The welfare of his animals is his responsibility, and I've rarely known a farmer or rancher who didn't take that responsibility seriously, and far beyond mere profit and loss.

Watching a stockman spend most of a day freeing an old cow from a bog or nursing a sick old ewe back to health may not make much sense to a corporate executive from a time/money standpoint, but there is some difference, I think, between manufacturing widgets in a New Jersey factory and being God's deputy.

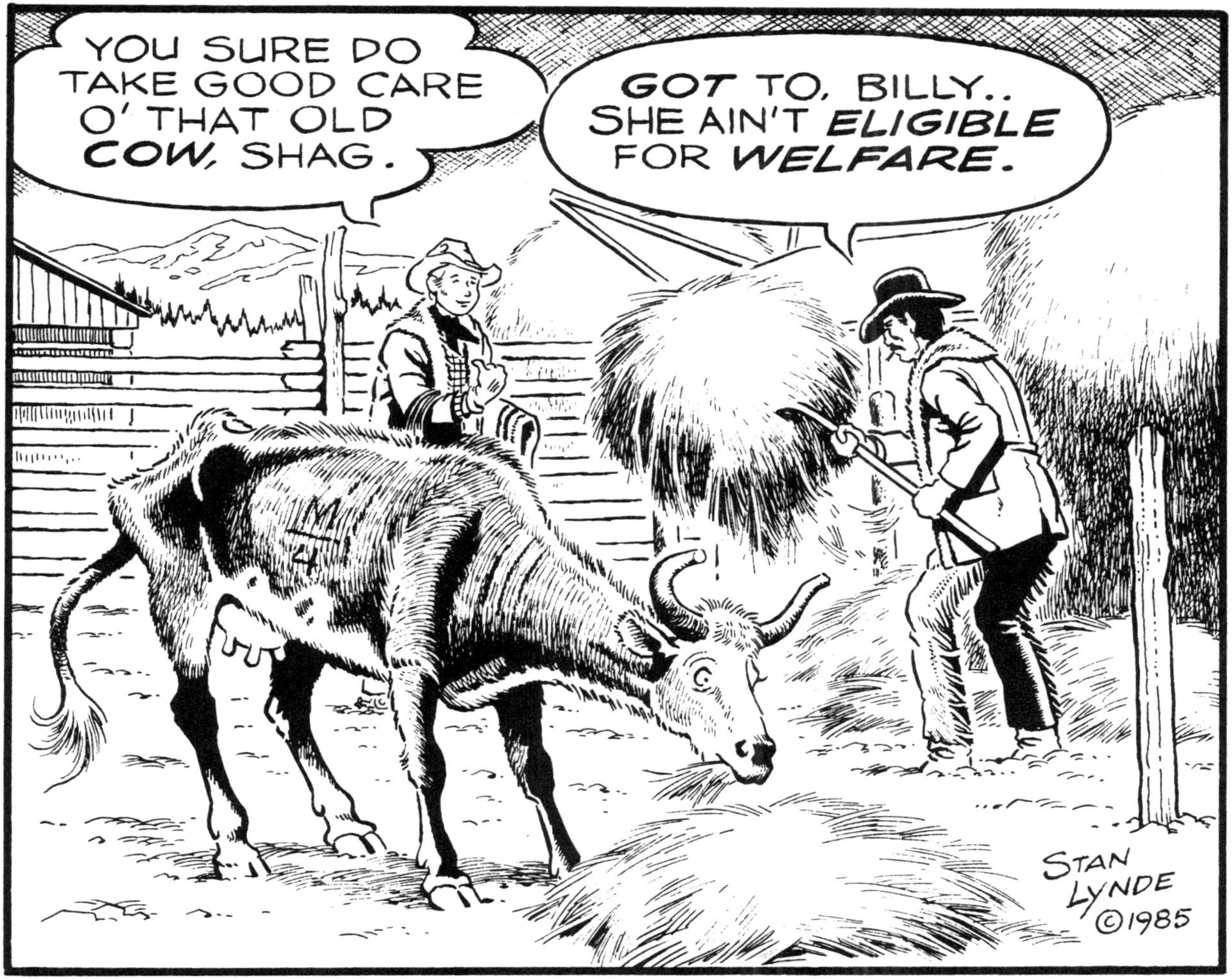
YOU SURE DO TAKE GOOD CARE O' THAT OLD **COW**, SHAG.
GOT TO, BILLY.. SHE AIN'T ***ELIGIBLE*** FOR ***WELFARE***.
STAN LYNDE ©1985

When Christmas rolls around and the merry chime of the cash register rings forth across the land, when we're urged to buy and charge and spend, and the credit card is king, I like to get back to the real reason we celebrate that special day.

The third chapter of John, verse 16, tells us why God did what he did on that first Christmas, nearly 2,000 years ago:

"For God so loved the world that he gave his only begotten Son, that whosoever believeth in him shall not perish but have everlasting life."

We didn't have to be *good* so Santa would bring us something, we didn't have to be likeable, or important, or influential so that people would bring us gifts. All we had to be was *people*.

God's Christmas present is for *everyone*.

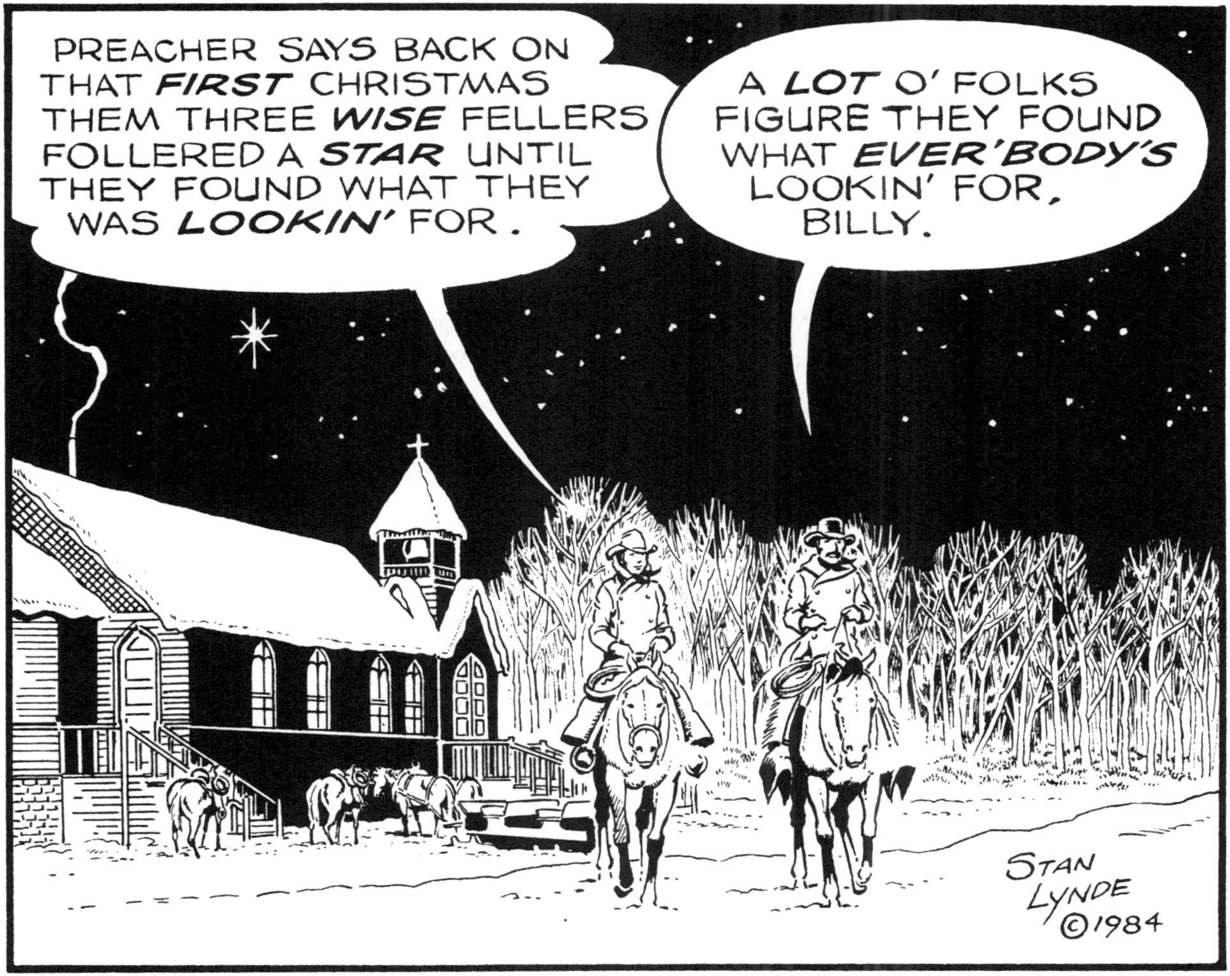
PREACHER SAYS BACK ON THAT FIRST CHRISTMAS THEM THREE WISE FELLERS FOLLERED A STAR UNTIL THEY FOUND WHAT THEY WAS LOOKIN' FOR.
A LOT O' FOLKS FIGURE THEY FOUND WHAT EVER'BODY'S LOOKIN' FOR, BILLY.
STAN LYNDE ©1984

It's only human to hope, and we do it every year.

New Year's Eve comes around and we all look ahead to a new year, make our resolutions of change, and try to believe in better days.

But our success and our happiness don't depend on better days, more money, or changed circumstances; our success depends on the changes we make in ourselves.

New life isn't a matter of putting up a new calendar, even though those clean, blank pages seem to promise new and unlimited possibilities; new life is a matter of changing the old *us*.

Happy New Year!

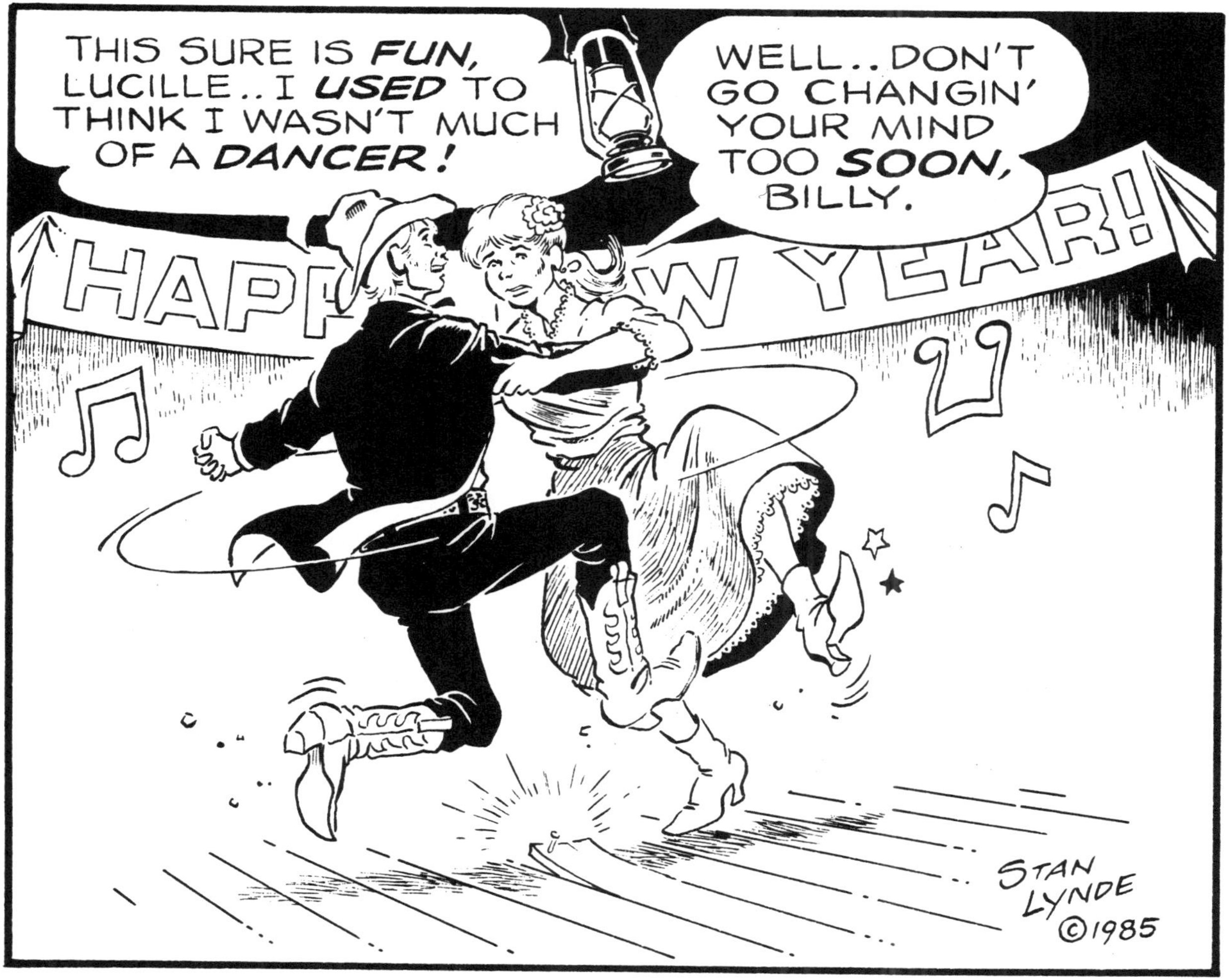
THIS SURE IS FUN, LUCILLE.. I USED TO THINK I WASN'T MUCH OF A DANCER!
WELL.. DON'T GO CHANGIN' YOUR MIND TOO SOON, BILLY.
HAPP W YEAR!
STAN LYNDE ©1985

When a man signs on to work cattle there are some occupational hazards that just go with the job, and he can't count on receiving much sympathy from his co-workers when they come up.

So when that big bay circle horse spooks at his shadow and piles you hard on the prairie gumbo, it's all in a day's riding. You're drawing a cowboy's pay and you're expected to live up to the job description.

It can be a hard life on a day like this, but you've learned by now to take the bitter with the sweet, and you wouldn't trade jobs with the richest broker on Wall Street.

Not *permanently,* anyway.

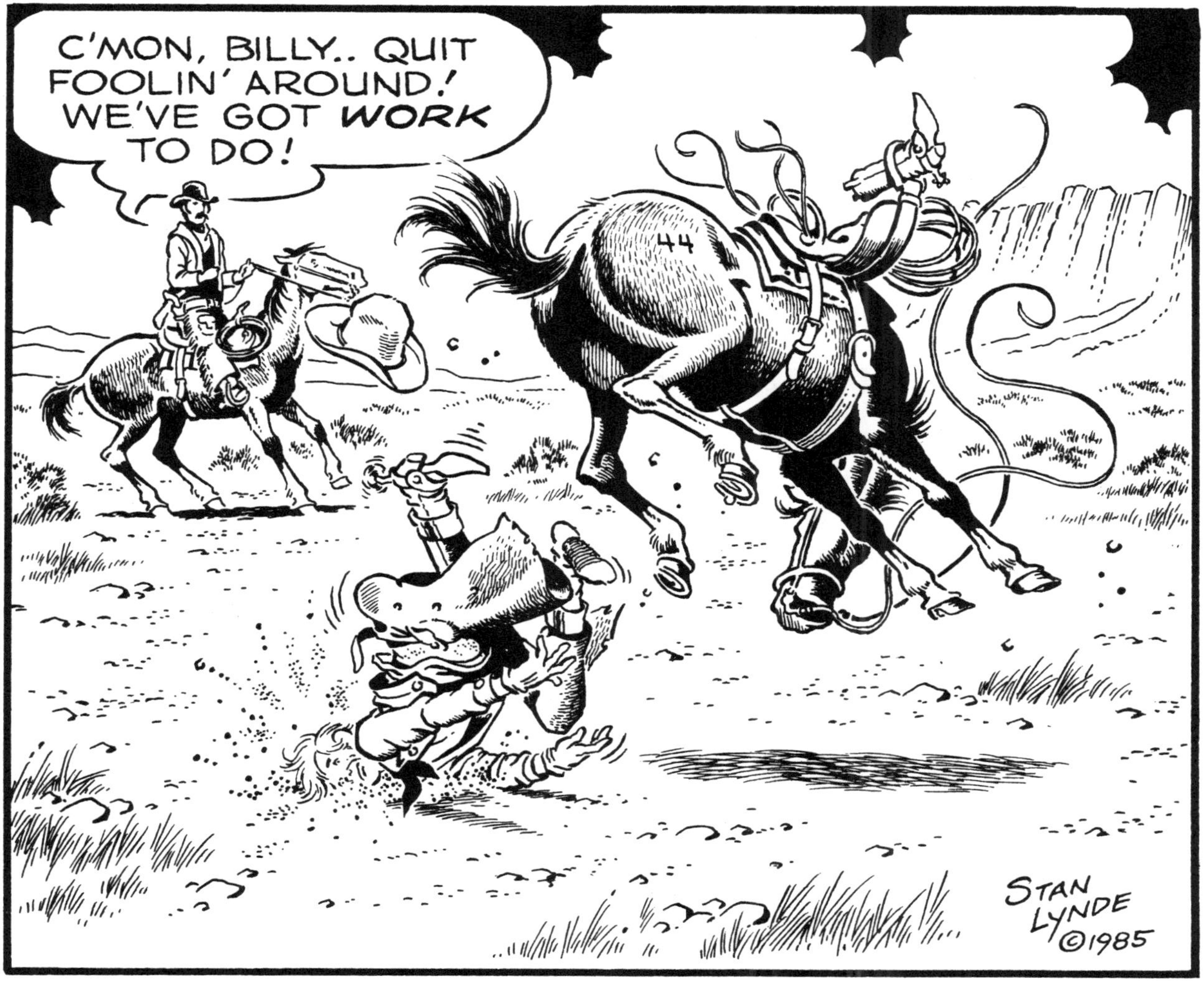
C'MON, BILLY.. QUIT FOOLIN' AROUND! WE'VE GOT **WORK** TO DO!
44
STAN LYNDE ©1985

Life *is* tough, at times; I believe the Almighty meant it to be, and if we all spent as much time learning from pain as we do trying to avoid it I think we'd gain a great deal more wisdom and contentment from our experience.

Shag's sympathy for the new-born calf is genuine, and he knows it faces still more hard knocks in the future, from predators and branding to blizzards and the slaughterhouse, but he's a realist.

He believes that life is worth living, in spite of tough times, and that being alive beats whatever's in *second* place.

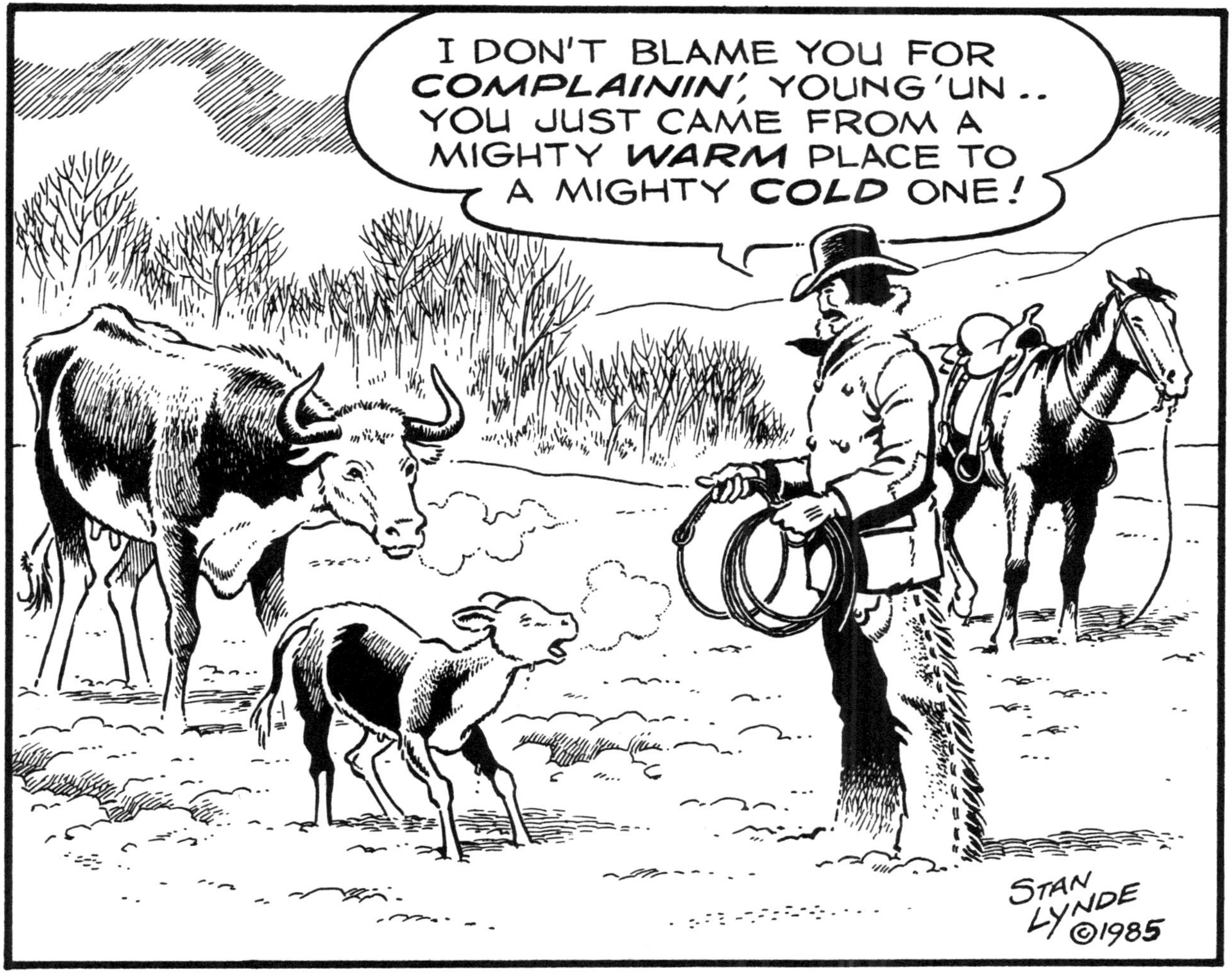
I DON'T BLAME YOU FOR COMPLAININ', YOUNG'UN .. YOU JUST CAME FROM A MIGHTY WARM PLACE TO A MIGHTY COLD ONE!
STAN LYNDE ©1985

The way of the world is filled with irony, and it doesn't take a great thinker to see that a lot of life just doesn't make much sense.

By all that's fair and just, America's farmers and ranchers should be among the world's most highly paid and respected people. Their products are basic and necessary for life on this hungry planet, and their industry and dedication have led to ever-increasing production on ever-decreasing acreage, and against the perils of predators, weather, crop disease, insects, imports, inflation, and politics.

Film stars and football players are better paid and honored by far, but you can't eat a movie--and astroturf makes a poor salad.

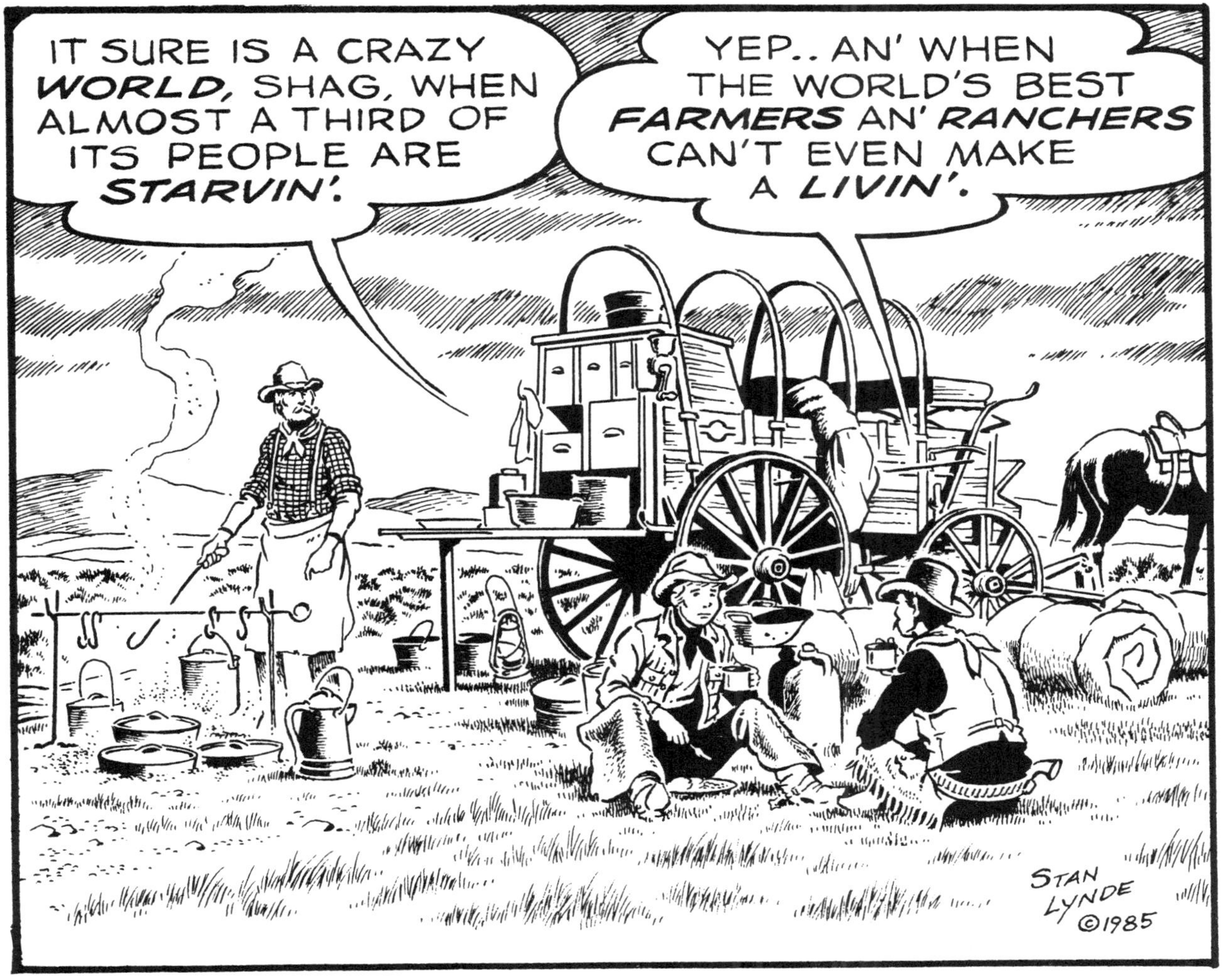
IT SURE IS A CRAZY *WORLD,* SHAG, WHEN ALMOST A THIRD OF ITS PEOPLE ARE *STARVIN'.*
YEP.. AN' WHEN THE WORLD'S BEST *FARMERS* AN' *RANCHERS* CAN'T EVEN MAKE A *LIVIN'.*
STAN LYNDE ©1985